25 Latino Craft Projects

ANA-ELBA PAVON
DIANA BORREGO

AMERICAN
LIBRARY
ASSOCIATION
Chicago
2003

D1288257

While extensive effort has gone into ensuring the reliability of information appearing in this book, the publisher makes no warranty, express or implied, on the accuracy or reliability of the information, and does not assume and hereby disclaims any liability to any person for any loss or damage caused by errors or omissions in this publication.

Project editor, Eloise L. Kinney

Composition by ALA Editions in Minion and Tekton using QuarkXPress 4.1 on a PC platform

Printed on 50-pound white offset, a pH-neutral stock, and bound in 10-point coated cover stock by McNaughton & Gunn

The paper used in this publication meets the minimum requirements of American National Standard for Information Sciences—Permanence of Paper for Printed Library Materials, ANSI Z39.48-1992. ∞

Library of Congress Cataloging-in-Publication Data

Pavon, Ana-Elba.
    25 Latino craft projects / by Ana-Elba Pavon and Diana Borrego.
        p. cm. — (Celebrating culture in your library)
    Includes bibliographical references.
    ISBN 0-8389-0833-0 (alk. paper)
        1. Children's libraries—Activity programs—United States.
    2. Children's libraries–Services to Hispanic Americans.
    3. Hispanic Americans—Social life and customs. 4. Latin America—Civilization—Study and teaching—United States.
    5. Multicultural education—Activity programs—United States.   I. Borrego, Diana.   II. Title.   III. Title: Twenty-five Latino craft projects.   IV. Series.
    Z718.2.U6P38 2002
    027.62'5—dc21   2002005750

Printed in the United States of America.

07   06   05   04   03   5   4   3   2   1

To Bibliotecas Para La Gente (the Northern California chapter of REFORMA). —D.B. and A.P.

To Fred and Julia Iltis and R.G., to whom I owe the achievement of my M.L.S. —D.B.

To J.C. y mi mami. —A.P.

Contents

ACKNOWLEDGMENTS   *vii*

GLOSSARY   *ix*

1 Latino Craft Programming and Planning   1

Craft Programming   *1*

Craft Planning   *2*

Using Recommended Books and Activities   *3*

2 Day of the Child/Day of the Book/Día de los Niños/Día de los Libros: April 30   5

Preschool Program: Straw Streamers   *6*

After-School Program: Cascarones   *6*

Family Program: Family *Códice*   *7*

Family Program: Paper Beads   *8*

Activities   *10*

3 Fifth of May/Cinco de Mayo: May 5   12

Preschool Program: Chiles on a String   *13*

After-School Program: Chile Pepper Magnet   *13*

After-School Program: Tin Art   *14*

Family Program: Oaxacan Sun   *18*

Family Program: Making *Gorditas*   *19*

Activities   *19*

4 Hispanic Heritage Month/Mes de la Herencia Hispana: September 15–October 15   21

Preschool Program: Flags   *21*

Brazil   *22*   Chile   *23*

Costa Rica   *24*   El Salvador   *25*

Guatemala   *26*   Honduras   *27*

Mexico   *28*   Nicaragua   *29*

After-School Program: Corn Husk Dolls   *30*

Family Program: Incan Headdress   *32*

Family Program: Incan Headband   *34*

Activities   *35*

5 Day(s) of the Dead/Día(s) de los Muertos: November 1 and 2   37

Preschool Program: Calavera Mask   *38*

After-School Program: Day of the Dead Skull   *40*

After-School Program: Day of the Dead *Papel Picado*   *41*

Family Program: Skeleton Puppet   *44*

Activities   *44*

6 Christmas/Navidad *48*

Preschool Program: Christmas Tree *49*

Preschool Program: Three Kings Silhouettes *51*

After-School Program: Ojos de Dios *54*

Family Program: Farolitos *56*

Family Program: Poinsettia Paper Flowers *57*

   Christmas Punch/*Ponche Navideño* Recipe *57*

Activities *58*

7 Everyday Crafts *59*

After-School Program: Paper Bag Piñata *59*

After-School Program: Papier-Mâché Balloon Piñata *62*

Family Program: Paper Flowers *62*

   Agua de Jamaica (Hibiscus Flower–Flavored Water) Recipe *64*

Sweet Tamales Recipe *65*

Salsa Recipe *65*

Activities *66*

APPENDIX: *Engrudo* and *Migajón*

   Engrudo/Glue Recipe *67*

   Migajón/Dough Recipe *67*

BIBLIOGRAPHY *69*

Acknowledgments

At the California Library Association Conference held in Oakland, California, November 14–17, 1998, the California Library Association's Services to Latinos Round Table and Bibliotecas Para La Gente (BPLG, the Northern California chapter of REFORMA) sponsored a Latino crafts program. The committee included Diana Borrego, Kate Connell, Sally Fuentes, Maria Mena, and Ana-Elba Pavon. The crafts were presented to a standing-room-only audience that reflected the great demand for Spanish services. The supplemental *Hispanic/Latino Crafts Resource Handbook* that was available at the presentation resulted in this book.

Thanks to Sandra Rios Balderama, Patrick Hogan, everyone at ALA Editions, and Bibliotecas Para La Gente for their contributions in making this book a reality.

The collections of the San Francisco Public Library, San José Public Library, and the Peninsula Library System were used for research and in choosing appropriate program materials. San Francisco's Mission Branch and San José's Biblioteca Latinoamericana were particularly instrumental in this endeavor, and we would like to thank everyone who has contributed to the acquisition and management of these two very special collections.

Glossary

aguas, flavored waters made out of seeds, powder, or fruit

aguinaldos, gifts

artesanias, folk art

atole, a drink

biscochitos, cookies

buñuelos, cookies

calaveras, skeletons and skulls

carne asada, steak

cascarones, decorated eggshells filled with confetti

cempázuchitl, marigold

ciguapa, a tribe of beautiful underwater people

códices, books made out of animal skin

cuetlaxochitl, overblooming flower

curandera, a healer

engrudo, glue

farolitos, small lanterns. *See also* luminarias

fiesta, party

gorditas, thick tortillas filled with all sorts of ingredients

huipiles, blouses

La Flor de Nochebuena, the Christmas Eve flower

La Llorona, the wailing woman searching for her children; also "the weeping woman"

La Novena de Navidad, Nine Days of Prayers before Christmas

Las Posadas, the reenactment of Mary and Joseph seeking shelter

luminarias, paper bags with candles inside; traditionally, small bonfires of stacked wood. *See also farolitos*

masa, dough

masa harina, masa flour

migajón, dough

Misa del Gallo, midnight mass; literally, "The Rooster's Mass"

ofrenda, altar

Ojos de Dios, God's Eyes

panicuas, straw weavings

papel picado, cut-paper art

pastorela, a play

ponche Navideño, Christmas punch

ponches, hot fruit drinks

tamalera, a pot specifically designed to cook tamales

tejocotes, a Mexican fruit

tilma, handmade cloak

CHAPTER 1

Latino Craft Programming and Planning

CRAFT PROGRAMMING

Fun literature-based programs introduce children to books, reading, and knowledge. Children learn through play, and children's librarians incorporate finger plays, songs, puppets, flannel-board stories, storytelling props, and crafts into programs where they read out loud to children. Educators, health providers, and others serving children and their literacy needs do likewise. Crafts reinforce story-time stories, songs, finger plays, and themes. Parents appreciate taking home something their child made, and the craft reminds them to come to other craft programs. In this book, librarians, educators, and others can introduce children to Latino culture via making Latino crafts.

With the exception of chapter 7, "Everyday Crafts," each of the following chapters focuses on a Latino holiday most likely to be celebrated by Latino communities in the United States. Libraries, schools, health services, businesses, and other agencies will be able to use each chapter's preschool (for children under six years old), after-school (for children over six years old), and family (for all ages) programs in their institutions.

Latino craft programs teach the importance of diversity and respecting different cultures. They also instill pride in members of the Latino community and give them a sense of belonging in both their community and their library. Some of you have growing Latino populations; you can use Latino craft programs as an outreach tool. Some of you have assimilated or mainstream Latino populations wishing to maintain their traditions. Some of you would like to expose non-Latino populations to Latino culture during a Latino holiday or multicultural event. Some of you have regular craft programs and welcome new material. All of us want to market our library collections, make our programming appeal to a wide range of audiences, and encourage children to read. We also want to attract new audiences. One way is by making Latino crafts part of our repertoire.

Artesanias, or folk art, are passed down from generation to generation by untrained artisans. Many traditional Latino *artesanias* date back so far, academics can only speculate as to their exact origin. Yet they are so common that they can be taken for granted by those who regularly create what is by definition a simple piece of folk art. Some families are well known for making a particular type of *artesania*. These families might work together for profit. They might work on their *artesania* throughout the calendar year, create seasonally for holidays and festivals, or take orders for special occasions.

Family, home, traditions, and children are very important to the Latino community, so whenever possible, host family programs that the entire family can attend together. Adults enjoy the crafts as much as the children and might even want to make their own! Some adults may also volunteer to help you or other children. It is important that the programs reflect Latino culture. Serve traditional foods and decorate. Get Latino members of your community involved in planning the activities. Ask Latino patrons, community members, businesses, groups, and clubs to volunteer or donate their goods or services. Someone might show you how to sing a traditional song, know of someone else who can help you, or do the program for you. Latinos in the audience can also share their experiences during the program. Make sure to promote the program bilingually and enlist the help of Spanish-language media—radio, television, and newspapers. Whenever possible, leave a telephone number where Spanish-speaking staff can give callers more information.

The public library experience can be intimidating to newcomers to the United States. Education and public libraries are not always readily available throughout Latin America, and people often fear things with which they are unfamiliar. To appeal to Latinos, public libraries and other agencies should offer them something with which they are familiar—aspects of their culture that they will recognize, such as language, music, or *artesanias*. These types of programs give Latinos a sense of pride and create a more welcoming environment. When Latinos recognize a place's value and feel comfortable there, they are more likely to return. As you build relationships, you can promote your other services at these programs or on an individual basis when the patrons return. Once they have a sense of belonging, Latinos will actively recommend your programs and services to their friends and extended families, resulting in a better-served community and more successful programs.

CRAFT PLANNING

Careful planning of craft programs can make the projects enjoyable for all, from start to finish. The following tips will help smooth the way for successful craft programs.

Promote Your Program

The best way to promote your Latino craft program is by word of mouth. Try to personally invite as many people to your event as possible because Latino communities respond best to personal invitations. Other ideas include writing press releases for both the English- and Spanish-language media—radio, television, and newspapers. If you have a relationship with public schools in your area, you can share posters and fliers with them. All materials should be bilingual to reach both English- and Spanish-speaking patrons. Ask a volunteer to make several of the crafts to serve as promotional displays in the library and at other places where children gather. Make sure to put up a sign that includes the name and date of the craft program so that people will know where the crafts came from and inquire about future programs. If the crafts are especially colorful or serve to celebrate an upcoming holiday, let the local newspapers know so they can send a photographer.

Finally, don't forget to announce your next program when you are finishing your current one. This is a good time to preregister children and adults for the next program.

Preregister Participants

Preregistering participants allows the host to limit the size of the group and purchase enough materials. Take the child's name and telephone number, and make a reminder call the day before the program. Make a waiting list in case there are cancellations. If someone does not come on the day of the program, there may be room for people who arrive, did not preregister, and are not on the waiting list. To be fair, however, keep track of the order in which the crafters arrive, so the ones waiting longest are the first to join the group.

On the other hand, many Spanish-services children's librarians recognize that they have to be accommodating when dealing with newcomer populations and try to avoid preregistration as much as possible. Planning the program is more of a challenge when one does not know the number of participants, but when providing outreach services to underserved communities, it is necessary to make things as easy as possible for the clientele.

Use Volunteers

Volunteers can be invaluable before, during, and after craft programs, so try to recruit them. Volunteers can free staff to work on other duties and in some cases are responsible for a program's continuity.

Crafts require preparation. Volunteers can do some preparation before the program or at any time at home. Volunteers can photocopy and precut patterns for younger children. They can put all the pieces together in an envelope, a plastic or paper bag, or with a paper clip. The day of the craft program, volunteers can prepare each craft station and craft area.

During the program, volunteers can pass out the craft and supplies, help children with their crafts, and handle complicated or potentially dangerous parts of the crafts.

After the craft, volunteers can help clean up.

Make a Sample

Make a sample of the craft in advance. This will familiarize you with the craft and help you plan. You can then display the sample during the program for the participants. Have a volunteer make several of them to help advertise the program or to raffle off as a prize for craft participants (see "Hold a Raffle" below).

Supervise the Crafters

Make sure that there is enough supervision for the craft. Arrange for staff or volunteers to be present. This is not as necessary when the children have an accompanying adult during the family programs. Remember to keep sharp objects and anything that can be swallowed, eaten, or cause damage away from small children.

Prepare the Craft Area

Think about cleaning up when preparing the craft area for the craft. If the craft might be messy, cover surface areas with newspapers or paper or plastic tablecloths. Put extra wastebaskets nearby as needed. Divide shared general supplies evenly. Put individual craft materials at each craft station, or plan how they will be distributed. Make sure extra materials are accessible in case the audience is larger than anticipated. Wear an apron, smock, or appropriate clothing in case you get dirty (or in case one of the participants gets you dirty!).

Create a Crafts Display

When the children finish their crafts, display them in the library, put up a sign with the program's name and date, and arrange for the craft owners to pick them up by taking their contact information. Encourage them to tell their family, friends, and teachers to come see their crafts at the library. This is a good opportunity for those who did not attend the program to visit the library. They will see what the library has to offer and possibly attend a future program. Make sure to have future program information available to hand out to inquiring patrons.

Hold a Raffle

Make several versions of the craft, and take extra care making them so that you can raffle them off as prizes to participants. Pass out numbered tickets to the participants, and pull the winning ticket from a hat. This is also an easy way to count participants for statistical purposes. In addition to all the benefits of having a raffle, the different versions give the children ideas to unleash their creativity in making their own crafts. You can also raffle donations such as books or cassettes or inexpensive trinkets related to the craft.

Evaluate

When the program is over, evaluate the different components. Think about what would have made the program run more smoothly and what should be changed the next time you do this program.

USING RECOMMENDED BOOKS AND ACTIVITIES

Every craft in this book is followed by a list of recommended books that are age-appropriate and related to the holiday or the craft or both. Similarly, each chapter ends with an activities section that includes songs, poems, and other materials that can be incorporated into the programming. These materials can be used in a variety of ways to enhance a craft program while showcasing reading and literature-based activities.

Plan a Crafts Story Time

Host a complete story-time program using the books and activities either before or after the craft portion of the program. Because the craft is usually the main attraction, it is advisable to do the story-time portion prior to the craft.

Family story times attract audiences of all ages—infants through grandparents—which makes choosing materials that will hold everyone's interest a challenge. In addition, many newcomers attend with their extended families, and you will want to encourage them to return. However, the feeling of success as multigenerational families start having fun can be extremely rewarding. The recommended books chosen for the family story times vary in length and appeal to all ages. Substitute preschool or after-school recommended books when programming for an audience of children who are older, younger, or who have wavering attention spans. Songs are usually a family story-time favorite, so be sure to include them.

Books get longer as the audience gets older, and if you tell the stories in two languages, it doubles the time spent on them, so after-school and bilingual story times might consist of only one or two books. In those cases, begin and end with a song, and consider adding a poem or other short activity.

Combine Longer Crafts with Other Activities

Although many of the crafts in this book can be completed in a relatively short period of time, others may take longer to complete if, for example, pasting or dough is involved. In those cases, the craft can become a two-day program or a long one-day program. When the craft requires some waiting, such as waiting for glue to dry, plan other activities accordingly. Deciding exactly what to do will depend on various factors such as the time allocated for the entire program, the amount of waiting time, whether the children need to clean up, and the location of the craft, reading, and cleanup areas.

If there is a short waiting time, read one book before the craft. During the wait, read poems and essays, sing songs, reinforce the book that was read by doing a book-related activity or asking questions, and have people share their experiences with the holiday or craft—there will be as many different traditions as there are people in Latino communities.

If there is a longer waiting time, do story time during the wait, incorporating the recommended books

with the songs, poems, and other materials. This might also be a good time to bring in a guest speaker to talk about his or her experiences with the holiday or the craft; ask a community member, Latino entrepreneur, master craftsperson, or museum or college representative. Someone in the community might be willing to display his or her personal collection of crafts in your library and talk about them during this time.

Incorporate Poetry with Crafts

Introduce poetry to children at a young age. Children naturally like rhymes and songs, so practice reading poetry with some sort of rhythm or beat. Have the children repeat poems with you. Children also love to laugh, so choose something funny. Children delight in discovering something that is just like them, so choose poetry that reflects their culture, traditions, and daily life.

Visual aids can bring the written word to life. Many of the poems in the picture-book format are beautifully illustrated with bright, bold, and appealing colors. Poems also make excellent flannel boards. Have the children assist you in the retelling by placing the figures on the flannel board. If there is time, make sure everyone gets a turn.

Use Music with Crafts

Songs are usually a story-time highlight, and although some of the community may be unfamiliar with reading and its value, they are familiar with songs and crafts. Make a flannel board out of a song. Put on a sound recording to lead the group during that portion of the program if necessary. Have a native speaker from the community teach you some songs, or ask a native speaker to lead the group in the singing. Many librarians sing a song or two between books, but if someone with an instrument is available, consider a longer sing-along complete with rhythm instruments for the children.

Crafts programs can be as simple or as elaborate as you like. With careful planning, they can incorporate a little bit of something—from stories to poetry to music—for everyone.

CHAPTER 2

Day of the Child/ Day of the Book

Día de los Niños/ Día de los Libros April 30

Many countries around the world celebrate Children's Day. The United Nations Children's Fund (UNICEF) celebrates it on April 23, and the United Nations celebrates it on November 20. For these countries, it is a day to focus on children. Such a day did not exist in the United States until recently.

In 1996, many teachers, librarians, and author Pat Mora started a movement in the southwestern United States to celebrate Day of the Child/Day of the Book/Día de los Niños/Día de los Libros in the United States on April 30, the date of Mexico's Children's Day. Thanks to their efforts, many schools, libraries, and organizations are now celebrating Día de los Niños/Día de los Libros in the United States.

Día de los Niños/Día de los Libros celebrates children, literacy, and the power of language. Many librarians and teachers celebrate Día de los Niños/Día de los Libros with bilingual story times and reading about different cultures. The emphasis is on celebrating all children no matter what language they speak. Children also enjoy making books and bookmarks and other activities. The activities all vary, but the important thing is that the activities focus on the children. Latinos are very family oriented, so it is important to include activities that all age groups can attend and enjoy. The books and activities in this chapter reflect these themes.

Some celebrations take place on April 30 or on a day close to it. Some celebrations last a week; some last a weekend. Large celebrations can include children's performers, culture groups, music, dance, puppets, crafts, health fairs, author visits, and book-character visits. Remember, it is a party, so don't forget the food and decorations.

Try to get your community involved during the planning stage. Ask government officials to issue a proclamation, and invite them to attend your activities. Local service agencies can distribute information about themselves at your event. Businesses can donate food, raffle prizes, and in-kind services. Larger corporations can sponsor the entertainment, or a school, class, or amateur can provide the entertainment. Local schools can also decorate, and teachers and older students can volunteer at your event. Invite an author or illustrator to attend, but if he or she cannot visit, maybe he or she can provide your library with an autographed door prize. And individual volunteers can also help make your event a success by assisting with all of the above.

Latinos from different countries are very familiar with Día de los Niños. Many have fond memories of activities that focused on children in their own countries. In the United States this day is an opportunity to introduce literacy to Latino families while celebrating children of all ethnic backgrounds and those who speak different languages. Focusing on the child is what makes this day important, so try the following programs, which celebrate childhood activities, family, language, and reading.

PRESCHOOL PROGRAM
Straw Streamers

Día de los Niños/Día de los Libros is a day to celebrate childhood. Many celebrations throughout Latin America celebrate with things children enjoy—their favorite foods, activities, and toys. Crafts are important to Latinos, and crepe paper is used for a variety of creations. Here, use crepe paper to make straw streamers that children can use for play.

Supplies

    straws

    crepe paper streamers

    invisible or transparent tape

Instructions

1. Cut the crepe paper streamers to the length of 1 foot.
2. Use about three different colors to make the streamer colorful.

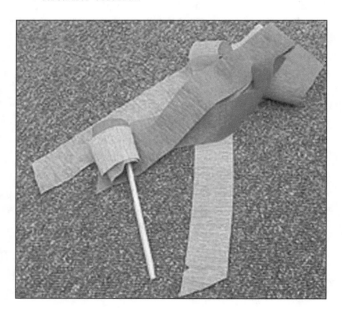

3. Tape the crepe paper to the top of the straw. The child can hold on to the bottom of the straw and wave it.

Recommended Books

Note: The bibliography at the end of the book provides complete information for each title.

Cisneros, Sandra. *Hairs/Pelitos.*

Guy, Ginger Foglesong. *¡Fiesta!*

Rohmer, Harriet, ed. "Enrique Chagoya." In *Just Like Me.*

Tabor, Nancy María Grande. *Somos un Arco Iris/We Are a Rainbow.*

AFTER-SCHOOL PROGRAM
Cascarones

Cascarones, decorated eggshells filled with confetti, are known in the southwestern United States, Mexico, and other parts of Latin America. Traditions for use vary. Some make *cascarones* only for Easter. Some make them every Sunday. In the United States, some families have a piñata and *cascarones* at their birthday parties and other festivities. The ceremony leading up to their use varies as well, but that is the one thing they have in common—they are all broken on top of someone else's head!

Supplies

    20 eggs

    5 ounces of confetti

    5 sheets of tissue paper (Craft, art, and gift tissue paper come in different sizes; any size will do.)

    colored markers

    invisible or transparent tape

    engrudo (glue) (*see* the appendix for the recipe—1 batch/100 eggs)

Instructions

Prepare steps 1 through 4 in advance.

1. Take a fresh egg and make a small hole at both ends.
2. Blow out the inside of the egg by placing your mouth on one of the openings.

3. Run water through the egg to clean it out.

4. Let the shell dry upside down overnight.

Prepare steps 5 and 6 in advance or have the children do as part of the program.

5. Cut tissue paper into 1″-long strips.

6. Another option is to create tissue paper cutouts with professional stamps or shape punches in addition to the 1″-long strips for decorating the egg in step 11. (Stamps and punches are available at office supply, drug, stationery, and craft stores in the office supply or photo-album and scrapbook section.) Make sure the paper cutouts are the right size to decorate an egg.

7. Fill the egg with prepared confetti.

8. Cover the egg holes with tape.

9. Cover the egg with *engrudo*.

10. Cover the egg with the 1″ strips of tissue paper. The *engrudo* makes the tissue paper stick to the egg.

11. Decorate the egg with colored markers, stickers, or tissue paper cutouts.

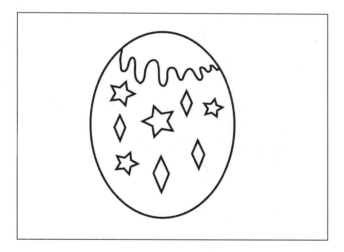

Recommended Books

Johnston, Tony. *Uncle Rain Cloud.*

Lachtman, Ofelia Dumas. *Pepita Talks Twice/Pepita Habla Dos Veces.*

Lomas Garza, Carmen. "Easter Eggs/Cascarones." In *In My Family/En Mi Familia.*

Mora, Pat. *The Rainbow Tulip.*

Mora, Pat. *Tomás and the Library Lady.*

FAMILY PROGRAM
Family *Códice*

The Aztecs produced several *códices* (codices), books made out of animal skin, that survived the Spanish conquest and destruction of Mesoamerican books. They documented genealogies, daily life activities, and history.

Use your codex as a picture album, a diary, or as a gift for a friend.

Supplies

2½ pieces of 8½″ × 11″ construction paper/child

1 piece of 8½″ × 11″ poster board/2 children

engrudo (glue) (*see* the appendix for the recipe—1 batch/100 books)

20-inch ribbon/child

safety scissors

Instructions

1. In advance, cut construction paper in half into 4¼″ × 11″ strips.

2. Fold each construction paper strip in half so that it measures 4¼″ × 5½″.

3. Take one folded strip, Folded Strip A, and insert one half of another folded strip, Folded Strip B, inside of it lengthwise, but first turn Folded Strip B backward, so that the crease faces up.

4. Open the top half of Folded Strip A while holding the inserted half of Folded Strip B to the bottom of Folded Strip A.

5. Use *engrudo* to glue the two touching pieces of paper together.

6. Fold Folded Strip B. It will now be Folded Strip A.

7. Repeat Steps 3 through 7 until all the paper is used or the desired length is reached.

8. Cut two pieces of poster board slightly larger than your folded paper for the outside covers.

9. Glue a piece of ribbon horizontally on both ends of your folded paper.

10. Glue the poster board pieces to the ends of your folded paper. The ribbon should be between the ends of the folded paper and the poster board pieces. The book will open somewhat like an accordion, and children can draw and write on both

sides of each page. The ribbon is used to tie the book shut once the children have finished their artwork.

Optional: Add more construction paper strips to increase the book's size. Make sure to do so in odd numbers, so that the book's two outside covers face the same direction.

Recommended Books

Elya, Susan Middleton. *Say Hola to Spanish.*

Libura, Krystyna. *What the Aztecs Told Me.*

Lomas Garza, Carmen. "Birthday Party." In *Family Pictures/Cuadros de Familia.*

Rohmer, Harriet. *Uncle Nacho's Hat/El Sombrero del Tío Nacho.*

FAMILY PROGRAM
Paper Beads

Beads are created and used for decoration in many cultures around the world. In Peru, the indigenous people make ceramic, stone, and metal beads. The hand-painted beads are then made into necklaces and other jewelry or sold individually so people can make their own jewelry. Here, different-colored paper is used to make the beads.

Supplies

8½″ × 11″ paper (bright colors)

safety scissors

glue

plastic coffee stirrers

Instructions

1. Cut triangles of paper from the pattern.
2. Make a thin line with the glue on one triangle, beginning at the center of the triangle's bottom wide end, continuing up the length of the triangle, and ending at the triangle's tip.
3. Place the coffee stirrer on the triangle so that it lines up at the bottom wide end of the triangle.
4. Begin rolling the paper tightly onto the plastic coffee stirrer.
5. Place the rolled-up bead on a metal tray to dry.
6. Slip dry beads off the plastic coffee stirrer.
7. String beads on thread or fishing wire to make a necklace or a bracelet.

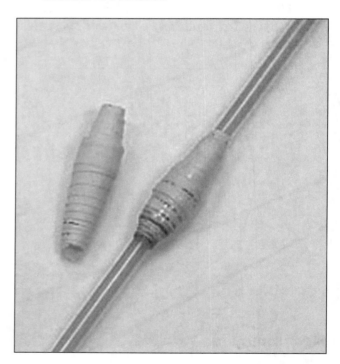

Recommended Books

Ancona, George. *Barrio: José's Neighborhood.*

Elya, Susan Middleton. *Say Hola to Spanish.*

Mora, Pat. *A Birthday Basket for Tía.*

Soto, Gary. *Chato's Kitchen.*

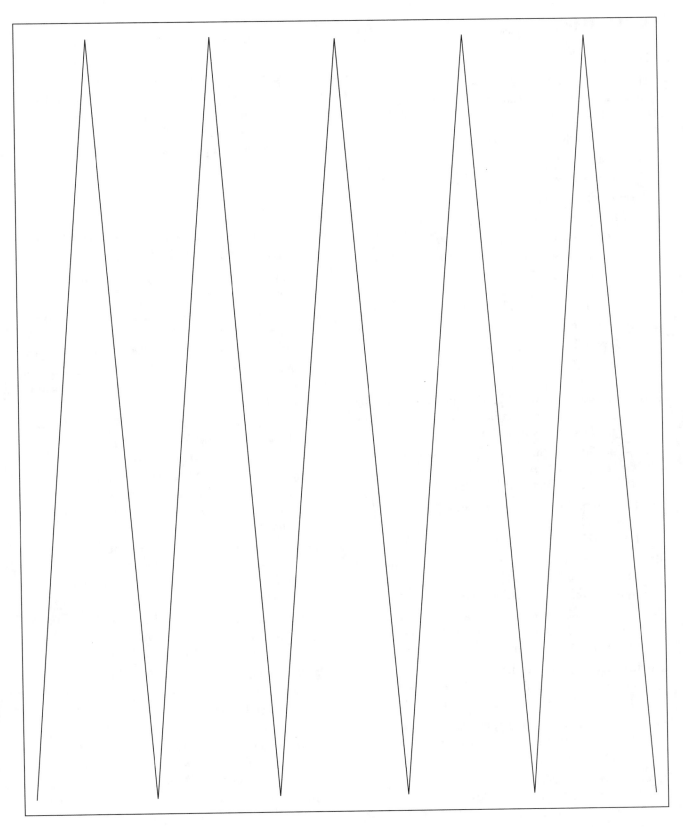

Triangle pattern

ACTIVITIES

Songs

"The Day of the Child and Book"
(Tune: "La Raspa/The Mexican Hat Dance")
by Ana-Elba Pavon

> The child, the child, the child *(clap, clap)*
> is what we celebrate *(clap, clap)*
> with books, with books, with books *(clap, clap)*
> on April thirtieth. *(clap, clap)*
> With pride, with pride, with pride *(clap, clap)*
> we speak our languages. *(clap, clap)*
> What fun, what fun, what fun *(clap, clap)*
> is the Day of the Child.
>
> And we'll share each other's culture
> and we'll read some good books
> and we'll speak different languages
> on the Day of the Child and Book.

Ada, Alma Flor, and Suni Paz. "Orgullo." On *Gathering the Sun: An ABC in Spanish and English (Spanish Songs)*. Del Sol Publishing. Compact disc.

Ada, Alma Flor, and Suni Paz. "Querer." On *Gathering the Sun: An ABC in Spanish and English (Spanish Songs)*. Del Sol Publishing. Compact disc.

Barchas, Sarah. "In Spanish, en Español." On *¡Piñata! And More! Bilingual Songs for Children*. High Haven Music NHM-109C. Audiocassette and book.

Barchas, Sarah. "It's Fun to Be Bilingual." On *¡Piñata! And More! Bilingual Songs for Children*. High Haven Music NHM-109C. Audiocassette and book.

Barchas, Sarah. "Languages We Speak." On *¡Piñata! And More! Bilingual Songs for Children*. High Haven Music NHM-109C. Audiocassette and book.

Barchas, Sarah. "¡Leamos! (Lets Read!)." On *¡Piñata! And More! Bilingual Songs for Children*. High Haven Music NHM-109C. Audiocassette and book.

Orozco, José-Luis. "Las Mañanitas." On *De Colores and Other Latin-American Folk Songs for Children*. Arcoiris Records. JL-20 CD Vol. 9. Compact disc.

Orozco, José-Luis. "Mi Familia." On *Diez Deditos—Ten Little Fingers & Other Play Rhymes and Action Songs from Latin America*. Arcoiris Records. JL-22 CD Vol. 12. Compact disc.

Paz, Suni. "Llega la Mañana (In the Morning)." On *ALERTA Sings & Songs for the Playground/Canciones para el Recreo*. Smithsonian Folkways Recordings SFW CD 45055. Compact disc.

Paz, Suni. "Los Vecinos (The Neighbors)." On *ALERTA Sings & Songs for the Playground/Canciones para el Recreo*. Smithsonian Folkways Recordings SFW CD 45055. Compact disc.

Poems

Ada, Alma Flor. "Orgullo/Pride." In *Gathering the Sun*.

Ada, Alma Flor. "Querer/Love." In *Gathering the Sun*.

Aguilar, Liz Ann Báez. "Growing Up." In *Love to Mamá*, ed. Pat Mora.

Alarcón, Francisco X. "Bilingual." In *From the Belly-button of the Moon and Other Summer Poems/Del Ombligo de la Luna y Otros Poemas de Verano*.

Alarcón, Francisco X. "Books." In *Angels Ride Bikes and Other Fall Poems/Los Ángeles Andan en Bicicleta y Otros Poemas de Otoño*.

Alarcón, Francisco X. "Family Recipe." In *Angels Ride Bikes and Other Fall Poems/Los Ángeles Andan en Bicicleta y Otros Poemas de Otoño*.

Alarcón, Francisco X. "My Grandma's Songs." In *Laughing Tomatoes and Other Spring Poems/Jitomates Risueños y Otros Poemas de Primavera*.

Alarcón, Francisco X. "My Grandmother Is an Angel." In *Angels Ride Bikes and Other Fall Poems/Los Ángeles Andan en Bicicleta y Otros Poemas de Otoño*.

Alarcón, Francisco X. "My Mother's Hands." In *Angels Ride Bikes and Other Fall Poems/Los Ángeles Andan en Bicicleta y Otros Poemas de Otoño*.

Alarcón, Francisco X. "Ode to Buena Vista Bilingual School." In *Iguanas in the Snow and Other Winter Poems/Iguanas en la Nieve y Otros Poemas de Invierno*.

Alarcón, Francisco X. "A Tree for César Chávez." In *Laughing Tomatoes and Other Spring Poems/Jitomates Risueños y Otros Poemas de Primavera*.

Alarcón, Francisco X. "Words Are Birds." In *Laughing Tomatoes and Other Spring Poems/Jitomates Risueños y Otros Poemas de Primavera*.

Arroyo, Rane. "My Tongue Is Like a Map." In *Love to Mamá*, ed. Pat Mora.

Carlson, Lori Marie, ed. "Grandpa Singing." In *Sol a Sol*.

Gatti, Gustavo. "Mama." In *Sol a Sol*, ed. Lori Marie Carlson.

Griego, Margot C., and Betsy L. Bucks. "Mama's Kiss." In *Tortillas para Mamá and Other Nursery Rhymes/ Spanish and English*, select. and trans. Sharon S. Gilbert and Laurel H. Kimball.

Herrera, Juan Felipe. "Mama's Mexican Clay Bowl, an Onion Is Born." In *Laughing Out Loud, I Fly*.

Herrera, Juan Felipe. "Uncle Beto Begins with Piloncillo." In *Laughing Out Loud, I Fly*.

Herrera, Juan Felipe. "When the Mail Carrier Discovered My Aunt." In *Laughing Out Loud, I Fly*.

Mora, Pat. "Abuelita's Lap." In *Confetti*.

Mora, Pat. "Castanet Clicks." In *Confetti*.

Mora, Pat. "Dancing Paper." In *Confetti*.

Mora, Pat. "Words Free as Confetti." In *Confetti*.

Soto, Gary. "Ode to Family Photographs." In *Neighborhood Odes*.

Soto, Gary. "Ode to My Library." In *Neighborhood Odes*.

CHAPTER 3

Fifth of May/ Cinco de Mayo
May 5

Although many mistake Cinco de Mayo (May 5) for Mexican Independence Day, it is in fact the anniversary of the Battle of Puebla, where a poorly armed Mexican militia defeated the French army. The capital of the state of Puebla, Puebla is located 65 miles southeast of Mexico City.

Mexico gained its independence from Spain on September 16, 1810. However, the years that followed included much turmoil, including the Mexican-American War and the Mexican civil war of 1858. Mexico suffered economically and borrowed money from other countries. After Benito Juárez was reelected president of the United States of Mexico in 1861, he called for a two-year moratorium on all foreign debts with a promise to resume payments thereafter. Spain, England, and France decided to intervene to get their payments. France was particularly interested because it planned to invade Mexico and establish French rule over Mexico under Archduke Maximilian of Austria.

On December 8, 1861, the European powers landed at Veracruz, Mexico. England and Spain withdrew their support when they discovered France's plan. Led by Napoleon Bonaparte's nephew, Leon Bonaparte, the French army advanced toward Mexico City in early April 1862. President Juárez ordered General Ignacio Zaragoza Seguin to hold back the French army at the city of Puebla. On May 5, 1862, the outnumbered Mexican militia and Zacapoaxtlas Indians hoped to stall the well-equipped French army to give Mexico City more time to fortify itself. Instead, they managed to win the battle.

A year later, Napoleon sent 30,000 troops to invade Mexico and installed Maximilian as its ruler. However, the victory of Puebla inspired the Mexicans to continue fighting. If they beat the French once, they could do it again. Sure enough, Maximilian was overthrown in 1867. In the meantime, Cinco de Mayo has come to symbolize Mexican nationalism.

Cinco de Mayo is a national holiday in Mexico, but it is celebrated more elaborately in the state of Puebla and the city of Puebla, where the battle took place. The battlefield is now a park with a statue of General Zaragoza Seguin. The city of Puebla celebrates Cinco de Mayo with a large patriotic parade.

Ironically, celebrations of Cinco de Mayo are more widespread and elaborate in the United States. Mexican American communities in states such as Texas, California, and Arizona celebrate with parades, fairs, mariachis, folkloric dancers, and authentic Mexican food. During the Chicano movement of the 1960s and 1970s, Cinco de Mayo grew in importance as a time for Mexican Americans to celebrate their patriotism, heritage, and culture. As the festivities have grown, they have come to include all Latinos living in the United States, giving all Latinos a sense of unity and ethnic pride.

PRESCHOOL PROGRAM
Chiles on a String

Chile peppers are a heavily used ingredient in Mexican cooking. They add flavor to traditional dishes and can be made into powder or eaten alone. Chile peppers are often hung on strings to dry. When cooking, one can just take some from the bunch hanging in the kitchen. Sometimes replicas are made out of plastic or ceramics for decoration. Try making your own out of paper.

Supplies

white construction or index paper

invisible or transparent tape

cotton twine (12″/string)

crayons

safety scissors

Instructions

1. Copy the chile pepper pattern onto white construction or index paper.
2. Color the chile peppers.
3. Cut out each individual chile pepper.
4. Tape each chile pepper on the cotton twine lengthwise so that each hangs on the string. Tape the ends of the string to the wall as a decoration.

Recommended Books

Note: The bibliography at the end of the book provides complete information for each title.

Alarcón, Francisco X. "Chile." In *Laughing Tomatoes and Other Spring Poems/Jitomates Risueños y Otros Poemas de Primavera.*

Behrens, June. *¡Fiesta! Cinco de Mayo.*

Reiser, Lynn. *Tortillas and Lullabies/Tortillas y Cancioncitas.*

Tabor, Nancy María Grande. *El Gusto del Mercado Mexicano/A Taste of the Mexican Market.*

AFTER-SCHOOL PROGRAM
Chile Pepper Magnet

As previously mentioned, chile peppers are used in many Mexican dishes. Chile peppers and the dishes in which they are cooked are not always spicy. In Mexico, it is customary to buy fruit on a stick topped with lime juice and sprinkled with dried, powdered chile. Chile candies are also very popular! These colorful magnets are fun to make and can serve as a reminder of the craft program when used.

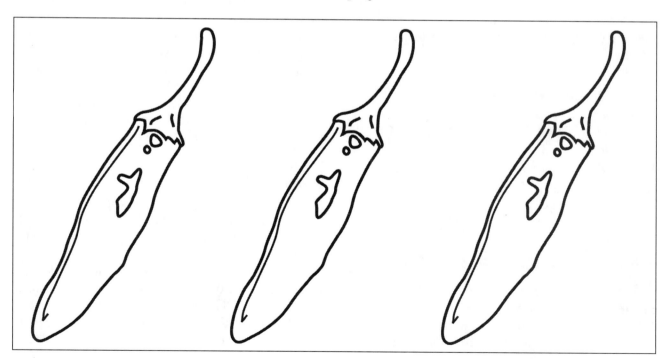

Supplies

migajón (dough) (*see* the appendix for the recipe—
1 batch/3 magnets)

green food coloring

fork

magnet strip

Instructions

1. Make *migajón* (dough).
2. Use food coloring to make it green.
3. Take a small amount of the dough and roll it so that one end is thicker than the other.
4. Curve the thin end to give the chile its shape.
5. Take a small ball of green dough to make the chile stem.
6. Place it on top of the chile and spread it out with the tip of a fork.
7. Flatten the back of the chile (to place the magnet on it), and let it dry overnight.
8. When dry, glue a magnet strip to the back of the chile.

Recommended Books

Alarcón, Francisco X. "Chile." In *Laughing Tomatoes and Other Spring Poems/Jitomates Risueños y Otros Poemas de Primavera.*

Alarcón, Francisco X. "Family Recipe." In *Angels Ride Bikes and Other Fall Poems/Los Ángeles Andan en Bicicleta y Otros Poemas de Otoño.*

Behrens, June. *¡Fiesta! Cinco de Mayo.*

Lomas Garza, Carmen. "Picking Nopal Cactus/ Piscando Nopalitos." In *In My Family/En Mi Familia.*

Mathew, Sally Schofer. *The Sad Night.*

Riehecky, Janet. *Cinco de Mayo.*

Soto, Gary. *Big Bushy Mustache.*

AFTER-SCHOOL PROGRAM
Tin Art

In ancient Mexico, the Mixtecs of Oaxaca (a Mexican state in the southern part of the country) were known as master craftsmen for their creations in gold and silver. The Aztecs too had gold and silver art and jewelry throughout their empire. After the Spanish conquest, the Spaniards stole their treasures and melted them down. Few items survived. The Spaniards forced the Indians to mine Mexico for all its precious metals and showed the Indians how to prepare the nonprecious metals previously unknown to them. Because it was then illegal for them to use precious metals, the Indians began using tin in their art. Today, tin is used in a variety of art forms. Mirrors, boxes, trays, jewelry, toys, Christmas ornaments, and much more are made out of tin and often painted with bright colors or left in its natural state.

In this adapted craft, you trace the following patterns onto small square tin sheets and display them as you wish. For instance, they can be framed with a traditional frame or with frame corners. Place a magnetic strip on the back and put them on the family refrigerator or school locker. Use a hole punch to punch a hole in them and use some decorative yarn or string to hang them. Use red, white, and green yarn for the Benito Juárez Silhouette and Mexican Flag Emblem as these are also the colors of the Mexican flag.

Benito Juárez Silhouette

Benito Juárez was born in the village of San Pablo Guelatao in 1806. When everyone in his family had died, he went to the city of Oaxaca at the age of twelve. He became a lawyer and later a judge. He was honest and stood up for the Indians. He became governor of Oaxaca in 1847 and president of Mexico in 1861. As president, he fought to give more power to the Indians and mestizos. He declared a moratorium on Mexico's debts that resulted in France attacking Mexico. When Mexico defeated the French in the Battle of Puebla, President Juárez declared Cinco de Mayo a national holiday.

Mexican Flag Emblem

According to Aztec legend, Quetzalcoatl was a god-hero who was changed into a bird and looked like a serpent. Defeated by an evil god, he would someday return to defeat his enemies. Legend promised the Aztecs a land where they would find an eagle sitting on a cactus, holding a snake in its beak. When the Aztecs found the eagle on a rock in the middle of Lake Texcoco, they settled there, which is where Mexico City is today. That is the significance behind the emblem on Mexico's national flag.

Benito Juárez pattern

Benito Juárez tin art

Mixtec Calendar Patterns

The Mixtecs lived in Oaxaca during the ninth century and spread over an extensive territory. They were an advanced culture that produced art, jewelry, and writing and studied astronomy. They created several *códices,* books made out of animal skin, that survived the Spanish conquest and destruction of Mesoamerican books. These books documented genealogies, daily life activities, and history. Their ideographs were so good that other peoples had the Mixtecs document their own *códices.* The origin of their writing is not known, and it is possible that Aztec writing is based on the Mixtec system. The Mixtecs had an exact calendar, and the designs reproduced here for making tin art are from that calendar.

Supplies

precut decorator foil squares (approximately 5″ × 5″) (The square sheets can be ordered in packets of one dozen squares from St. Louis Crafts, Inc.: phone, 1-314-638-0038; website, <http://www.stlouiscrafts.com>.)

pencils or medium-point pens

newspaper

Instructions

1. Make copies of the patterns.
2. Padding is needed to trace the design onto tin. Make sure there are several layers of newspaper under the tin before you trace the design so that the image shows nicely.
3. Trace the patterns on the foil with the pencil or pen.

Recommended Books

Corpi, Lucha. *Where Fireflies Dance/Ahí Donde Bailan las Luciérnagas.*

Gollub, Matthew. *The Twenty-Five Mixtec Cats.*

Lomas Garza, Carmen. "Eagle with Rattlesnake." In *Magic Windows/Ventanas Mágicas.*

Palacios, Argentina. *¡Viva México! A Story of Benito Juárez and Cinco de Mayo.*

Salinas, Bobbi. *The Three Little Pigs/Los Tres Cerdos.*

Bird

Drawing by Paul Gonzalez

Mexican Flag Emblem

Buzzard

Dog

Catrina *(Posada)*

Frog

Calavera

Pancho *(Posada)*

All drawings on this page by Paul Gonzalez

FAMILY PROGRAM
Oaxacan Sun

The Sun and the Moon are frequently seen throughout Mexican folk art. Perhaps this can be attributed to the Aztecs, who lived in Mexico before the Spaniards. The ancient Aztec city of Teotihuacán, about 28 miles from Mexico City, was much larger than any European city during that time, and two pyramids were dedicated to the Sun and the Moon. The Aztecs kept a very accurate calendar and had many beliefs concerning the life cycle. They watched the Sun's activity carefully and offered it human sacrifices because they believed this would keep it shining. A giant carved stone disk known as the Sun Stone hung at the Temple of Huitzilopóchtli in Tenochtitlán, the capital of the Aztec empire, where Mexico City now stands. It is believed that the face at its center represents the sun god. Found by those making a new subway system in Mexico City after having been buried when the Spaniards came, the Sun Stone is a source of cultural pride among Mexicans. Children will enjoy making and decorating suns of their own.

Supplies

> *migajón* (dough) (*see* the appendix for the recipe— 1 batch/sun)
>
> pencil
>
> yellow food coloring (if desired)
>
> yarn (for hanging the suns)

Instructions

1. Make the *migajón* (dough).
2. Add yellow food coloring if desired.
3. Divide 1 batch of dough in half.
4. Use your hands to spread the dough into a circle 2″ in diameter with one-half of the dough.
5. Use the other half of the dough to make slanted triangles that will form the sun's rays.
6. Attach the triangles to the sun by wetting the wide edge of the triangle and joining the pieces with your fingers.
7. Pinch the clay to form the eyes, the nose, and the mouth.
8. Use a pencil to make a hole at the top for hanging purposes.
9. Let dry.

Optional two-day program: If you have room, provide small pieces of cardboard or ask participants to bring their own. Have the children put their names on the piece of cardboard where their sun is drying. The children can return to paint their suns on the second day of this craft program when the suns are dry.

Display ideas: Because this craft lends itself to hanging, take advantage if you have hanging space and display these suns in the library. Have a party with snacks. After the children put yarn through their completed suns, decide where to display them— and don't forget to tell the crafters to invite their friends and family!

Recommended Books

Ada, Alma Flor. *The Lizard and the Sun.*

Ehlert, Lois. *Moon Rope/Un Lazo a la Luna.*

Gollub, Matthew. *The Moon Was at a Fiesta.*

Johnston, Tony. *The Tale of Rabbit and Coyote.*

Johnston, Tony. "Where Are They Now?" In *My Mexico/México Mío.*

Mora, Pat. *The Night the Moon Fell.*

Rohmer, Harriet, ed. "Elly Simmons." In *Just Like Me.*

FAMILY PROGRAM
Making *Gorditas*

The indigenous people of Mexico believed corn to be sacred and had special ceremonies for their corn gods. Corn is used in a variety of ways and is a main ingredient in tortillas. Tortillas are made from ground corn and look similar to pancakes. They can be fried to make crispy tacos; baked to make enchiladas; filled or covered with meat, cheese, beans, or lettuce; or buttered and eaten with a meal, as one might eat buttered bread with a meal.

Preparing a dish in the library requires a bit of extra work, both before and after. But the rewards are many—even the toughest outreach groups are often tempted by the delicious smells and the fun of creating food. Here is a recipe for making *gorditas*—thick tortillas filled with all sorts of ingredients.

Supplies

4 cups of *masa harina* (*masa* flour, found in Latino markets and delis) to make 20 *gorditas*

3 to 4 cups of water

1 cup of cooked refried beans

½ cup of grated cheese

¼ head of lettuce sliced into thin pieces

3 medium-sized tomatoes cut into small pieces

salsa (*see* chapter 7, "Everyday Crafts," for the recipe)

electric grill for cooking the *gorditas*

Instructions

1. Prepare *masa harina* by following the instructions on the package or buy prepared *masa* (dough) from a Mexican store. The *masa* will be used to make the *gorditas*.

2. Prepare the ingredients that will be used to fill the *gorditas* in advance—cooked refried beans, grated cheese, lettuce, tomatoes, and salsa.

3. Make sure the participating family members wash their hands.

4. Give each participant a small portion (approximately golf-ball size) of the *masa*.

5. Demonstrate how to place the *masa* ball between your hands and flatten it out by moving the ball from hand to hand until it is approximately ½" thick.

6. Place the *gordita* on the grill to cook until you can lift it cleanly off the grill. Turn the *gordita* over and repeat.

7. The *gordita* is ready when it is light and airy. The middle will swell.

8. Let the *gordita* cool off.

9. Cut an opening on the side of the *gordita* wide enough to stuff the *gordita* with its ingredients.

10. You might want to serve a traditional drink with the *gorditas* (*see* chapter 6 for a recipe for Christmas punch and chapter 7 for a recipe for *Agua de Jamaica*). You can make them as part of the program, in advance, or purchase them at a restaurant or Mexican store.

Recommended Books

Alarcón, Francisco X. "Tortilla." In *Laughing Tomatoes and Other Spring Poems/Jitomates Risueños y Otros Poemas de Primavera.*

Chavarría-Cháirez, Becky. *Magda's Tortillas/Las Tortillas de Magda.*

Johnston, Tony. "Corn." In *My Mexico/México Mío.*

Kimmel, Eric A. *The Runaway Tortilla.*

Lomas Garza, Carmen. "Deer." In *Magic Windows/Ventanas Mágicas.*

Lomas Garza, Carmen. "Little Tortillas for Mother." In *Magic Windows/Ventanas Mágicas.*

Paulsen, Gary. *The Tortilla Factory.*

ACTIVITIES

Songs

"To Honor the 5th of May"
(Tune: "If You're Happy and You Know It")
by Ana-Elba Pavon

> To honor the 5th of May, clap your hands.
> To honor the 5th of May, clap your hands.
> To honor the 5th of May, when Puebla said, "Go away"
> To honor the 5th of May, clap your hands.

To honor the 5th of May, stomp your feet,

To honor the 5th of May, stomp your feet,

To honor the 5th of May, when Puebla said,
      "Go away"

To honor the 5th of May, stomp your feet.

To honor the 5th of May, shout, "¡Viva, México!"

To honor the 5th of May, shout, "¡Viva, México!"

To honor the 5th of May, when Puebla said,
      "Go away"

To honor the 5th of May, shout, "¡Viva, México!"

Ada, Alma Flor, and Paz, Suni. "México." On *Gathering the Sun: An ABC in Spanish and English (Spanish Songs)*. Del Sol Publishing. Compact disc.

Barchas, Sarah. "Cinco de Mayo." On *¡Piñata! And More! Bilingual Songs for Children*. High Haven Music NHM-109C. Audiocassette and book.

Orozco, José-Luis. "Benito Juárez." On *Fiestas/Holidays: Canciones para Todo el Año*. Arcoiris Records. JL-18 CD Vol. 6. Compact disc.

Orozco, José-Luis. "5 de Mayo." On *Fiestas/Holidays: Canciones para Todo el Año*. Arcoiris Records. JL-18 CD Vol. 6. Compact disc.

Orozco, José-Luis. "La Raspa." On *Diez Deditos—Ten Little Fingers & Other Play Rhymes and Action Songs from Latin America*. Arcoiris Records. JL-22 CD Vol. 12. Compact disc.

Orozco, José-Luis. "Tortillitas." On *Diez Deditos—Ten Little Fingers & Other Play Rhymes and Action Songs from Latin America*. Arcoiris Records. JL-22 CD Vol. 12. Compact disc.

Paz, Suni. "Tortitas, Tortitas (Cakes, Cakes)." On *ALERTA Sings & Songs for the Playground/ Canciones para el Recreo*. Smithsonian Folkways Recordings SFW CD 45055. Compact disc.

Poems

Ada, Alma Flor. "México/Mexico." In *Gathering the Sun*.

Alarcón, Francisco X. "Cinco de Mayo." In *Laughing Tomatoes and Other Spring Poems/Jitomates Risueños y Otros Poemas de Primavera*.

Alarcón, Francisco X. "From the Bellybutton of the Moon." In *From the Bellybutton of the Moon and Other Summer Poems/Del Ombligo de la Luna y Otros Poemas de Verano*.

Gonzalez, Maya Christina. "I Honor My Great-Grandmother Refugio Morales." In *Honoring Our Ancestors,* ed. Harriet Rohmer.

Quintero, Henry. "Making Tortillas." In *Sol a Sol,* ed. Lori Marie Carlson.

CHAPTER 4

Hispanic Heritage Month/Mes de la Herencia Hispana

September 15– October 15

The time period from September 15 to October 15 is known in the United States as Hispanic Heritage Month/ Mes de la Herencia Hispana. Coincidentally, many Latin American countries declared their independence during this time. For instance, on September 16, 1810, Miguel Hidalgo y Costilla, a parish priest, proclaimed the famed *Grito de Dolores*—calling for Mexicans to govern themselves—which began the armed struggle for Mexican independence. On September 18, 1810, the criollo leaders of Santiago, Chile, announced they would govern themselves. On September 15, 1821, Costa Rica, El Salvador, Guatemala, Honduras, and Nicaragua joined together in declaring their independence from Spain (following the Spanish Revolution of 1820). Finally, on September 7, 1822, Don Pedro I, heir to the Portuguese throne, declared Brazil's independence and became its emperor a few months later.

In 1968, Congress passed a law authorizing the president of the United States to proclaim the week including September 15 and 16 as "National Hispanic Heritage Week." The people of the United States would observe this week with appropriate ceremonies and activities honoring those of Hispanic heritage. U.S. Air Force Colonel Gil Coronado partnered with the Congressional Hispanic Caucus to campaign for expanding this week to a month. In 1988, Congress passed a law expanding the week to a month. The president of the United States is now authorized to proclaim the month of September 15 through October 15 "National Hispanic Heritage Month."

Although not all Latin American countries moved toward independence during these dates, Hispanic Heritage Month has come to include all Hispanics regardless of country of origin. Cities put on parades, churches put on festivals, and schools recognize all Hispanics in their activities. This is a time to honor Latinos and learn about Latino culture, and the following programs and activities are excellent ways to celebrate Hispanic Heritage Month.

PRESCHOOL PROGRAM
Flags

Although Hispanic Heritage Month is a time to learn more about Hispanic culture, only some Latin American countries took steps toward independence during this month. Their flags are represented here.

The Central American countries of Costa Rica, El Salvador, Guatemala, Honduras, and Nicaragua have a shared history because they were all part of the United Provinces of Central America. The current flags of these countries pay homage to the United Provinces of Central America flag that flew from 1823 to 1839, primarily by using its blue and white colors. Many of the current flags look similar because they were based on the United Provinces of Central America flag.

All the flags in this section are made of construction paper and use one 18″ × 12″ piece of construction paper as the flag's foundation. Other pieces are listed under the supplies for each flag. Prepare them in advance. This activity requires quite a bit of cutting, so you might need more volunteer or staff time than usual to prepare this craft. If the flag has a coat of arms, it is printed backward for photocopying. Some of the emblems have been stylized and simplified for artistic purposes. The children will color the coat of arms and glue all the pieces in place.

This craft ties in well with the "Raise the Flag" song that appears in this chapter's "Activities" section. While the flags are drying, read a story and teach the children the song, so that when the flags are dry, the children can wave their flags high in the air during the song's chorus.

BRAZIL

The Brazilian flag bears the motto "Ordem e Progresso" ("Order and Progress"). The green and golden-yellow colors symbolize forests and minerals. Portugal colonized Brazil, and blue and white are Portugal's historic colors.

Supplies

    one 18″ × 12″ green construction paper sheet

    one 9″ × 8½″ piece of yellow or golden yellow construction paper in the shape of a parallelogram (a four-sided figure with less than 90-degree angles)

    one 5½″ (circumference) blue construction paper circle

    one ½″ × 6″ white construction paper semiarched strip

    27 white construction paper stars (small, medium-sized, and large)

    blue marker or crayon

    glue sticks

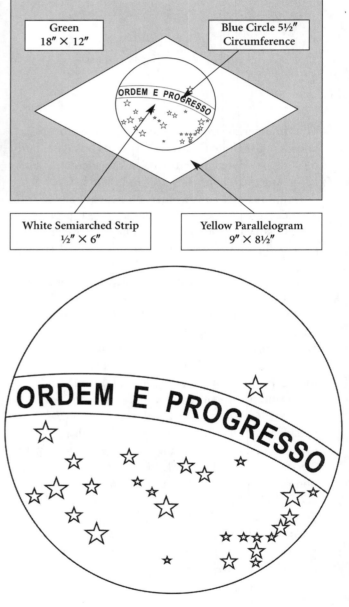

Instructions

1. Glue the yellow parallelogram-shaped construction paper in the middle of the green construction paper.

2. Glue the blue construction paper circle in the middle of the parallelogram shape.

3. Glue the semiarched white strip of construction paper above the middle of the blue circle.

4. Glue one white star above the white strip of paper. Glue the rest of the white stars below the white strip of construction paper. Write "ORDEM E PROGRESSO" in blue capital letters on the white strip of paper.

CHILE

The white star on Chile's flag stands for progress and honor. The red stands for the blood of heroes, the white for the snow of the Andes, and the blue for the sky.

Supplies

    one 18″ × 12″ white construction paper sheet
    one 18″ × 6″ red construction paper piece
    one 6″ × 6″ blue construction paper piece
    one white construction paper star 3″ across
    glue sticks

Instructions

1. Glue the red construction paper on the bottom half of the white construction paper.

2. Glue the piece of blue construction paper on the top left corner of the white construction paper.

3. Glue the white star in the middle of the blue construction paper in the left corner.

COSTA RICA

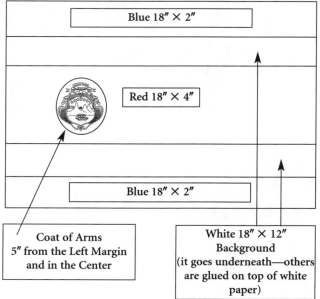

Blue 18″ × 2″

Red 18″ × 4″

Blue 18″ × 2″

Coat of Arms
5″ from the Left Margin
and in the Center

White 18″ × 12″
Background
(it goes underneath—others
are glued on top of white
paper)

Costa Rica's state flag, used by the government, was adopted in 1848. The coat of arms shows volcanoes, the Caribbean Sea, and the Pacific Ocean. Each star represents a province.

Supplies

one 18″ × 12″ white construction paper sheet

two 18″ × 2″ blue construction paper pieces

one 18″ × 4″ red construction paper piece

copy of the coat of arms on white paper

glue sticks

crayons

Instructions

1. Color the coat of arms with crayons.

2. Mark the left side of the white construction paper at 2″, 4″, 8″, and at 10″.

3. Glue one piece of blue construction paper on the top of the white construction paper.

4. Glue the other piece of blue construction paper on the bottom of the white construction paper.

5. Glue the red construction paper between the 4″ and 8″ marks.

6. Glue the colored coat of arms on the red strip of construction paper, approximately 5″ from the left margin and in the center.

EL SALVADOR

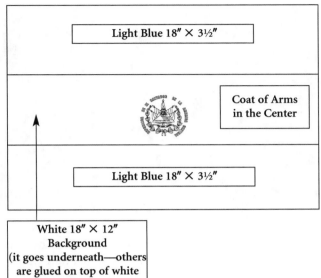

El Salvador's flag was adopted in 1912. The blue stripes represent unity, the white symbolizes peace, the triangle stands for equality, and the flags represent the Central American nations that made up the United Provinces of Central America.

Supplies

one 18″ × 12″ white construction paper sheet

two 18″ × 3½″ light blue
    construction paper pieces

copy of the coat of arms on white paper

glue sticks

crayons

Instructions

1. Color the coat of arms with crayons.

2. Glue one piece of light blue construction paper on the top of the white construction paper.

3. Glue the other piece of light blue construction paper on the bottom of the white construction paper.

4. Glue the colored coat of arms in the center, between the two light blue construction paper pieces.

GUATEMALA

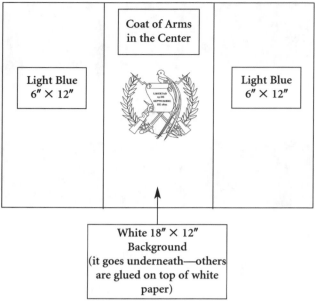

Coat of Arms
in the Center

Light Blue
6″ × 12″

Light Blue
6″ × 12″

White 18″ × 12″
Background
(it goes underneath—others
are glued on top of white
paper)

The flag of Guatemala was adopted in 1871. The two blue stripes represent the Pacific and Atlantic Oceans, which border the country. The coat of arms bears Guatemala's national bird, the quetzal bird, and the scroll bears the date independence was declared.

Supplies

one 18″ × 12″ white construction paper sheet

two 6″ × 12″ light blue construction paper pieces

copy of the coat of arms on white paper

glue sticks

crayons

Instructions

1. Color the coat of arms with crayons.

2. Glue one piece of light blue construction paper on the left side of the white construction paper.

3. Glue the other piece of light blue construction paper on the right side of the white construction paper.

4. Glue the colored coat of arms in the center, between the two pieces of light blue construction paper.

LIBERTAD
15 DE
SEPTIEMBRE
DE 1821

HONDURAS

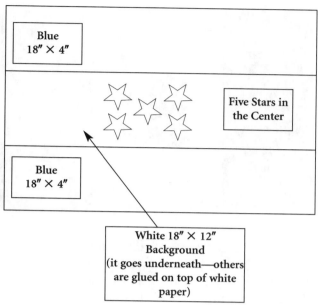

Blue
18″ × 4″

Five Stars in
the Center

Blue
18″ × 4″

White 18″ × 12″
Background
(it goes underneath—others
are glued on top of white
paper)

The Honduras flag was adopted in 1866. The five stars represent the nations that formed the United Provinces of Central America.

Supplies

> one 18″ × 12″ white construction paper sheet
>
> two 18″ × 4″ blue construction paper pieces
>
> 5 approximately 2″ × 2″ blue construction paper stars
>
> glue sticks

Instructions

1. Glue one piece of blue construction paper on the top part of the white construction paper.

2. Glue the other piece of blue construction paper on the bottom part of the white construction paper.

3. Glue the five blue stars in the center of the 18″ × 12″ white construction paper.

MEXICO

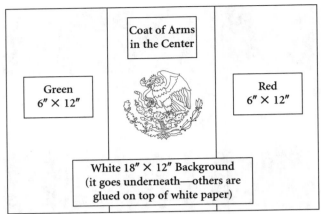

	Coat of Arms in the Center	
Green 6″ × 12″		Red 6″ × 12″
	White 18″ × 12″ Background (it goes underneath—others are glued on top of white paper)	

The Mexican flag represents the history of Mexico by combining three different traditions: the indigenous, the colonial and Hispanic heritage, and the independence movement. The coat of arms, an eagle standing on a cactus plant and devouring a snake, represents the place where the Aztec's god told them to settle.

The white color represents the purity of the Catholic religion, the green symbolizes the independence from Spain, and the red stands for the support the Spaniards born in Mexico provided to the movement.

Instructions

1. Color the coat of arms with crayons.
2. Glue the green construction paper on the left side of the white construction paper.
3. Glue the red construction paper on the right side of the white construction paper.
4. Glue the colored coat of arms in the center, between the green and red construction paper.

Supplies

one 18″ x 12″ white construction paper sheet

one 6″ x 12″ green construction paper piece

one 6″ x 12″ red construction paper piece

copy of the coat of arms on white paper

glue sticks

crayons

NICARAGUA

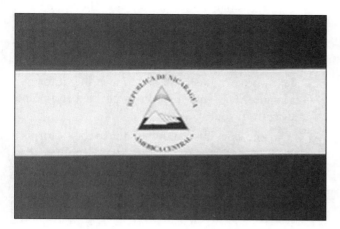

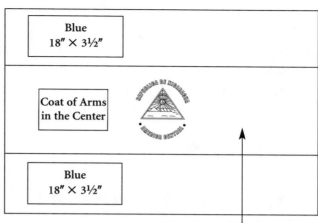

Nicaragua's flag was adopted in 1908. The volcano in the coat of arms represents the former United Provinces of Central America; the triangle stands for equality, the rainbow for peace, and the cap for liberty.

Supplies

one 18″ × 12″ white construction paper sheet

two 18″ × 3½″ blue construction paper pieces

copy of the coat of arms on white paper

glue sticks

crayons

Instructions

1. Color the coat of arms with crayons.

2. Glue one piece of the blue construction paper on the top of the white construction paper.

3. Glue the second piece of blue construction paper on the bottom of the white construction paper.

4. Glue the colored coat of arms in the center of the white construction paper.

Recommended Books

Note: The bibliography at the end of the book provides complete information for each title.

Dorros, Arthur. *Isla.*

Machado, Ana Maria. *Niña Bonita.*

Rohmer, Harriet, ed. *Honoring Our Ancestors.*

Viesti, Joe, and Diane Hall. *Celebrate! In Central America.*

Winter, Jeanette. *Josefina.*

AFTER-SCHOOL PROGRAM
Corn Husk Dolls

Corn was important to Mexico even in ancient times. Kernels of corn more than 9,000 years old have been found. Indians thought corn was sacred, and they had special ceremonies for corn gods. Corn is enjoyed as a vegetable and is also an important ingredient in Mexican cooking. It is used to make tortillas, which are eaten alone or used in many Mexican dishes, such as tacos, enchiladas, and quesadillas. After shucking the corn, instead of throwing away the corn husks, one can use them for cooking tamales—*masa* filled with meat or other ingredients and cooked in corn husks *(see chapter 7 for a recipe for Sweet Tamales)*—or for creating corn husk dolls.

Supplies

> Corn husks (Corn husks can be purchased in Latino grocery stores or in the "spices" or "Hispanic" sections of supermarkets.)

Instructions

1. Soak corn husks in warm water for at least 15 minutes or until flexible.
2. Shake water off corn husks and pat dry with towel or cloth.
3. Take one corn husk and flatten it so that it forms a triangle. Make sure the narrow pointed end points away from you.
4. Repeat step 3 with another corn husk and stack it directly on top of the first corn husk.
5. With a small piece of corn husk, tie the narrow pointed ends together approximately 2″ from the top.

6. Turn the husks inside out, and fold the wide ends over the small tied piece so that the wide piece opens up. This will become the head.
7. Take a small strip of corn husk and tie it around the husk an inch below the fold to create a head.
8. Take one corn husk and flatten it so that it forms a triangle. Make sure the narrow pointed end points away from you.
9. Take one corn husk and flatten it so that it forms a triangle, but make sure the narrow pointed end points *toward* you. Place it on top of the corn husk from step 8.

Arms tied securely (front)

Arms tied securely (back)

10. Roll up the two corn husks from step 9 lengthwise. These will become the arms.

11. Have the doll's head face you. The corn husks below the head are the body. Divide the body by lifting the front half of the corn husks (the side facing you) from the back half.

12. Place the arms between the front and back halves to form a T.

13. Hide the ends of the small strips used to tie the head by tucking them under the body.

14. Take another small strip of corn husk and tie the body securely below the arms, creating a waist.

15. Trim arms to desired length.

To make boy dolls: Split the body in the middle for pants and tie each leg near the bottom with small strips of corn husk.

Hair variation: To make a doll with hair, repeat step 4 (putting three corn husks together in same direction). Then, when you divide the body in step 6, leave the middle piece of corn husk loose. Tear it into strips for hair.

Recommended Books

Alarcón, Francisco X. "Ode to Corn." In *Laughing Tomatoes and Other Spring Poems/Jitomates Risueños y Otros Poemas de Primavera.*

Casteneda, Omar S. *Abuela's Weave.*

Jaffe, Nina. *The Golden Flower.*

McConnie Zapafer, Beatriz. *Fiesta!*

Stevens, Jan Romero. *Carlos and the Cornfield.*

FAMILY PROGRAM
Incan Headdress

Around A.D. 1100, Quechua-speaking Incas founded the city of Cuzco. The Incas were very organized, and their careful planning was crucial in their conquering land. The vast Incan empire grew tremendously and at one point included parts of Peru, Ecuador, Bolivia, Chile, and Argentina.

The Incas worshipped many gods. They considered themselves "children of the sun." The Sun was their most powerful god, and they were grateful to the Sun for the light and food it provided them. They built temples to the Sun. They also built temples to the Moon, which provided light during the night. Eclipses of the Sun and the Moon frightened them very much. The Incas felt eclipses were warnings that bad things were about to happen.

The Incas believed that they should go to war to conquer the world for their sun god. All able-bodied men were required to give military service, but only those who could be spared from a village served. A warrior's family was taken care of by the community in his absence. The Incas planned their tactics carefully, and most of the time, they conquered others through negotiation. If the other people surrendered peacefully, they were usually allowed to live as they had previously. If the other people did not surrender, the Incas tried such nonviolent means as spies and bribery to coerce them into surrendering.

Though violence was a last resort, Incan warriors were very disciplined and prepared to fight. Their jackets were strong enough to protect them against attack while allowing the warrior room for movement. They threw various weapons and wore protective helmets.

The following crafts are based on Incan helmets and elaborate feathered headdresses. The headdress is a two-day project because the items need time to dry, so plan activities accordingly.

Supplies

newspaper and newspaper cut into long strips

engrudo (glue) (*see* the appendix for the recipe—1 batch/10 headdresses)

balloon (balloon size 9) or a plastic bowl (the size of a child's head)

feathers (optional)

6 to 8 sheets of tissue paper per headdress (Origami paper can be used instead of tissue paper, but it is generally more expensive, and you will need more per headdress.)

glue gun

Note: Professionally made shape cutters, craft punches, and hand punches are available to cut paper in various shapes. You can use them to decorate *papel picado* (cut-paper art) projects (*see* chapter 5, "After-School Program: Day of the Dead *Papel Picado*"), and save the cutouts for this project. You can also make cutouts specifically for this project in advance or have the children participate during the craft project.

Instructions

1. Roll two sheets of newspaper lengthwise to form a tube.
2. Take long strips of newspaper wet with *engrudo* and wrap them around the tube to hold it together. Only one layer is necessary.
3. Bring ends together to form a crown.
4. Fold one end in order to place it inside the other open end.
5. Repeat instruction number 2, but wrap only around the ends. This will hold the crown together.
6. Use a bowl or round balloon to create a papier-mâché half dome. Use three or four layers of newspaper strips wet with *engrudo* to form the dome and to make it strong enough to stand upright.

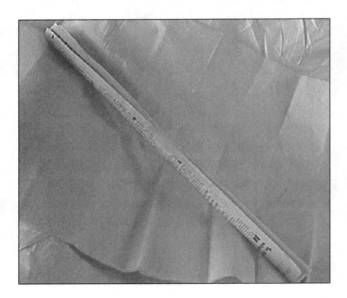

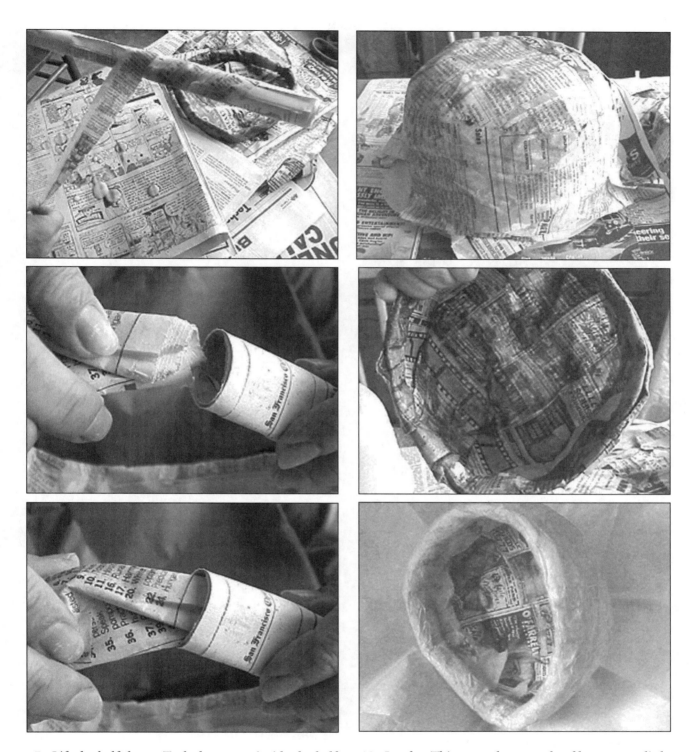

7. Lift the half dome. Tuck the crown inside the half dome.

8. Let dry overnight.

9. Cover the dome with tissue paper wet with *engrudo*. A minimum of three layers is necessary to hide the newspaper print.

10. Let dry. This may take a couple of hours or as little as half an hour in direct sunlight.

11. When the dome is dry, use a glue gun to attach feathers to the top of the dome if desired. Once dry, cover the bottom end of the feathers with strips of tissue paper wet with *engrudo* to hold them in

place. Decorate with tissue paper or origami cut-outs if desired.

FAMILY PROGRAM
Incan Headband

The Incan headband is a colorful craft that can be worn or used for decoration.

Supplies

> newspaper and newspaper cut into long strips
>
> *engrudo* (glue) (*see* the appendix for the recipe—1 batch/20 Incan headbands)
>
> 4 to 6 sheets of tissue paper per headband (Origami paper can be used instead of tissue paper, but it is generally more expensive, and you will need more per headband.)
>
> glue gun

Note: Professionally made shape cutters, craft punches, and hand punches are available to cut paper in various shapes. You can use them to decorate *papel picado* (cut-paper art) projects (*see* chapter 5, "After-School Program: Day of the Dead *Papel Picado*"), and save the cutouts for this project. You can also make cutouts specifically for this project in advance or have the children participate during the craft project.

Instructions

1. Roll two sheets of newspaper lengthwise to form a tube (*see* step 1 under the headdress instructions above).
2. Take strips of newspaper wet with *engrudo* and wrap them around the tube to hold it together. Only one layer is necessary (*see* step 2 under the headdress instructions above).
3. Choose either Method 1 (to form a crown) or Method 2 (to form a crown with two ends crossed).
4. Cover with tissue paper (desired color) wet with *engrudo*. A minimum of three layers of tissue paper is necessary to hide the newspaper print.
5. Let dry. This may take a couple of hours or as little as half an hour in direct sunlight.
6. When dry, use a glue gun to attach feathers or small versions of paper flowers (*see* Method 1 below; *see also* chapter 7, "Everyday Crafts," for "Family Program: Paper Flowers"). Once dry, cover the bottom end of the feathers with papier-mâché. Decorate with tissue paper or origami paper cutouts if desired (*see* Method 2 below).

Method 1: Bring both ends together to form a crown. Fold one end and place it inside the other open end (*see* steps 3 and 4 under the headdress instructions above). Take strips of newspaper wet with *engrudo* and wrap it around the tube to hold it together.

Incan headband (Method 1) with paper flower

Method 2: After steps 4 and 5 above, bring both ends together so that they overlap and cross one another, creating a crown with two ends up. Tie in place with string.

Incan headband (Method 2) with paper cutouts

Recommended Books

Alvarez, Julia. *The Secret Footprints.*

Ancona, George. *Fiesta U.S.A.*

Mohr, Nicholasa, and Antonio Martorell. *The Song of el Coquí and Other Tales of Puerto Rico.*

Rohmer, Harriet. *Uncle Nacho's Hat/El Sombrero del Tío Nacho.*

Wing, Natasha. *Jalapeño Bagels.*

ACTIVITIES

Songs

"Raise the Flag"
(Tune: "La Bamba")
by Ana-Elba Pavon

Every September and October,
Every September and October, we remember
When many Latino countries,
When many Latino countries during September
Gained liberty, gained liberty.

Raise the flag, raise the flag, raise the flag.

Every September and October,
Every September and October,
These countries share their language and culture,
Their language and culture.
It's their Hispanic heritage, heritage.

Raise the flag, raise the flag, raise the flag.

Every September and October,
Every September and October,
Celebrate with Latino food and tradition,
Latino food and tradition,
To remember the victory, victory.

Raise the flag, raise the flag, raise the flag.

Barchas, Sarah. "Hispanic Americans." On *¡Piñata! And More! Bilingual Songs for Children.* High Haven Music NHM-109C. Audiocassette and book.

Barchas, Sarah. "The 16th of September." On *¡Piñata! And More! Bilingual Songs for Children.* High Haven Music NHM-109C. Audiocassette and book.

Orozco, José-Luis. "16 de Septiembre." On *Fiestas/Holidays: Canciones para Todo el Año.* Arcoiris Records. JL-18 CD Vol. 6. Compact disc.

Poems

Alarcón, Francisco X. "Ode to Corn." In *Laughing Tomatoes and Other Spring Poems/Jitomates Risueños y Otros Poemas de Primavera.*

Alarcón, Francisco X. "A Tree for César Chávez." In *Laughing Tomatoes and Other Spring Poems/Jitomates Risueños y Otros Poemas de Primavera.*

Argueta, Jorge. "Language of the Birds." In *A Movie in My Pillow/Una Película en Mí Almohada.*

Argueta, Jorge. "Pupusas." In *A Movie in My Pillow/Una Película en Mí Almohada.*

Argueta, Jorge. "Voice from Home." In *A Movie in My Pillow/Una Película en Mí Almohada.*

Chapra, Mimi. "Mi Mamá Cubana." In *Love to Mamá,* ed. Pat Mora.

Essays

Crespo, George. "I Honor My Grandfather Antonio Nuñez." In *Honoring Our Ancestors,* ed. Harriet Rohmer.

Lomas Garza, Carmen. "Deer." In *Magic Windows/Ventanas Mágicas.*

Websites

Celebrate Hispanic Heritage! Hispanic History in the Americas <http://teacher.scholastic.com/hispanic/history.htm>

This interactive site gives time lines of Hispanic history.

Education World—Lesson Planning: Celebrate Hispanic Heritage Month <http://www.education world.com/a_lesson/lesson023.shtml>

Besides providing a lesson plan and activities for children, this site also links to related sites.

CHAPTER 5

Day(s) of the Dead/ Día(s) de los Muertos

November 1 and 2

Latinos in the United States and throughout Latin America celebrate the Day(s) of the Dead/Día(s) de los Muertos by remembering and honoring their ancestors in different ways. The Day of the Dead celebration is when the dead return to visit their family and friends on Earth. Many of the current rituals and customs have roots in the pre-Hispanic cultures of Mesoamerica and were celebrated throughout the year based on the fact that death was not to be feared but part of a journey. Life was a time of suffering, and death was when you woke up. When the Spanish conquistadors came and tried to establish Christianity, they brought new ideas of death, including heaven, hell, and purgatory.

Because the customs of the indigenous people were so powerful and had been in practice for so long, these traditions became intertwined with the rituals of Christianity. All the saints of the Roman Catholic Church are commemorated on All Saints' Day, November 1. All Souls' Day, November 2, is the designated time to pray for the souls of departed baptized Christians believed to be in purgatory. These two dates coincided with the Quecholli celebration honoring warriors that took place during the month of November on the Julian calendar. This fusion became the Day of the Dead celebration, where the souls of children are honored on November 1, and the adult souls are honored on November 2.

Today, this Indo-Hispanic holiday is celebrated differently in different places. Many states, cities, and towns in Mexico have unique observances and customs. Throughout the rest of Latin America, celebrations might include going to church, visiting the grave, cleaning it, and leaving offerings. Sometimes festivities are held at the cemetery, and sometimes they are held down the road from the cemetery.

In Mexico, the living prepare for the arrival of the dead in advance by cooking elaborate meals, creating banners cut from tissue paper, and baking a special "bread of the dead." Toys and cartoons depict skeletal images doing everyday things, thus mocking death and finding humor in it. Children eat candy skulls with their names on them. They also build *ofrendas* (altars) at home, graves, or business establishments. The *ofrendas* may be decorated with religious symbols, candles, photographs, favorite foods, favorite drinks, and marigolds. The marigold *(cempázuchitl)* is the flower of the Day of the Dead, symbolizing the regeneration of life. Black, white, pink, yellow, and gold are the Day of the Dead colors.

Regardless of where the Day of the Dead is celebrated, throughout Latin America and the United States this is a time for Latinos to remember their ancestors and celebrate life.

PRESCHOOL PROGRAM
Calavera Mask

Skeletons and skulls (*calaveras*) are common motifs of the Day of the Dead because the dead visit the living during these days. This is a happy occasion, and death is not feared but accepted as part of the life cycle. During the celebrations death is mocked, and what better way to do so than with a cheerful *calavera* mask?

Supplies

    white construction paper

    safety scissors

    thin elastic or ribbon

    hole punch

Instructions

1. Photocopy or trace the pattern onto the construction paper.

2. Cut out the eyes, nose, and teeth beforehand for the younger children; older children can cut their own.

3. Punch out one hole on each edge of the mask at eye level.

4. Use the holes next to the eyes to tie the ribbon or elastic to hold the mask on the child's face.

Recommended Books

Note: The bibliography at the end of the book provides complete information for each title.

Chumba la Cachumba. Illus. Carlos Cotte.

Johnston, Tony. *Day of the Dead.*

Krull, Kathleen. *Maria Molina and the Day of the Dead.*

Luenn, Nancy. *A Gift for Abuelita/Un Regalo para Abuelita.*

Viesti, Joe, and Diane Hall. *Celebrate! In Central America.* (*See* the section on the Day of the Dead.)

AFTER-SCHOOL PROGRAM
Day of the Dead Skull

This craft is a *migajón* (dough) variation on the traditional Day of the Dead Mexican sugar skulls *(calaveras)*, where clay molds are used to make skulls out of sugar. Sheep, pigs, hearts, shoes, and miniature plates of enchiladas are also made out of sugar for the Day of the Dead. Sometimes chocolate is used to make the skulls, but sugar skulls decorated with lots of bright colors are most common.

Master sugar-skull makers pass down the skills and the molds used to make sugar skulls from generation to generation within the family. It is a difficult process that requires heating sugar at extremely high temperatures. The molds come in different sizes, and many are old and very difficult to acquire. The artisan selling the skulls can write your name across the sugar skull's forehead upon request.

This variation is not edible and is undecorated.

Supplies

migajón (dough) (*see* the appendix for the recipe—1 batch/2 skulls)

round-tip tool (modeling clay tool or a pestle)

Instructions

1. Take dough and roll it into a small egg-shaped ball.

2. Press egg-shaped ball against a flat board to form a flat bottom for the skull.

3. Use your hands to press in both sides of the skull to form the cheekbones.

4. Use a round-tip tool to make the eye sockets.

5. In the center and below the eyes, make two small indentations for the nostrils.

6. Let dry.

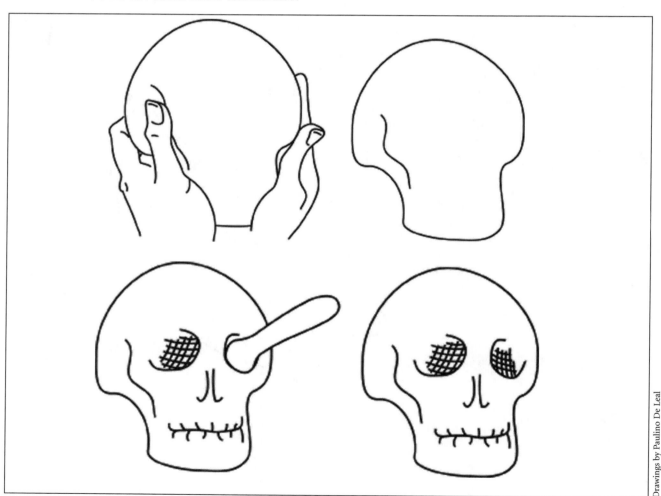

Drawings by Paulino De Leal

Recommended Books

Anaya, Rudolfo. *Maya's Children.*

Ancona, George. *Pablo Remembers.*

García, Richard. *My Aunt Otilia's Spirits/Los Espíritus de Mi Tía Otilia.*

Hoyt-Goldsmith, Diane. *Day of the Dead.*

Kimmel, Eric A. *The Witch's Face.*

Lasky, Kathryn. *Days of the Dead.*

Levy, Janice. *The Spirit of Tío Fernando/El Espíritu de Tío Fernando.*

Luenn, Nancy. *A Gift for Abuelita/Un Regalo para Abuelita.*

AFTER-SCHOOL PROGRAM
Day of the Dead *Papel Picado*

Tissue paper came to Mexico in the seventeenth or eighteenth century. Before that, paper was cut in Europe with scissors to create designs. Mexicans continued this tradition. It is customary to create paper banners made of cut tissue paper tied together on a string. These banners may hang over the street during a festival, at indoor or outdoor parties or weddings, in doorways, or any place or occasion imaginable.

The folds and cuts determine the banner's design. Make random cuts using the traditional Day of the Dead colors of black, white, pink, yellow, and gold to decorate, or use the following skeleton and grave pattern.

Supplies

> 1 20″ × 26″ gift tissue paper/2 paper banners (Use any of the following Day of the Dead colors: black, white, pink, yellow, and gold.)

safety scissors

paper clips

pencil

eraser

small pieces of scrap paper

garbage cans

string (if hanging multiple paper banners on one string)

glue sticks (if hanging multiple paper banners on one string)

Preparation

1. Cut each 20″ × 26″ sheet of gift tissue paper in half so that it measures 20″ × 13″. One 20″ × 13″ sheet makes one paper banner.

2. Photocopy one skeleton and grave pattern for each paper banner. (*See* pattern on page 42.)

   Note: This pattern shows only half of the skeleton and grave images. Placing the pattern on a folded paper edge, cutting the paper, and unfolding the paper reveals the full images.

3. This craft results in lots of small pieces of cut paper. Plan to use as many garbage cans as you can and position them strategically.

Instructions

1. Place one 20″ × 13″ gift tissue paper on a flat surface so that it measures 20″ horizontally and 13″ vertically.

2. Fold the cut 20″ edge over 2″ (where the string can be placed later for hanging purposes; *see* "Stringing Multiple *Papel Picado* Paper Banners" below). Folding the cut edge gives the *papel picado* maker the option of having a clean straight bottom edge by leaving the uncut edge alone.

3. Accordion pleat the paper by folding it vertically every 3″.

4. Place the pleated paper on a flat surface vertically with the 2″ folded edge, created in step 2, farthest away from you.

5. Fold and unfold the 2″ folded edge, creating a crease, and do not cut above the crease.

6. Take the pleated paper's bottom edge and fold to the 2″ folded edge crease, created in step 5. Unfold, and make sure that the fold created a crease in the middle of the pleated paper. The crease divides the pleated paper in half and is the reference point for placement of the skeleton and grave pattern in step 7.

7. Center the skeleton and grave pattern vertically on the pleated paper by making sure that the skeleton is on the top half of the pleated paper and that the grave is placed on the bottom half of the pleated paper. Remember to leave room at the top and bottom edges when centering the skeleton and grave pattern. Place the pattern on the *folded* vertical edge of the pleated paper.

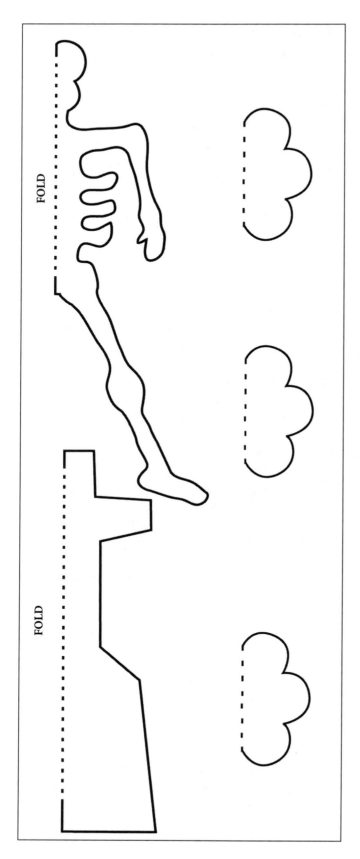

8. To keep it in place, you may want to paper clip the pattern to the *folded* vertical edge of the pleated paper, or use a pencil to lightly trace the pattern onto the *folded* vertical edge of the pleated paper.

9. Use scissors to cut the pattern out of the pleated paper's *folded* vertical edge. Make sure the paper stays folded and that the pattern does not move to prevent distorted images. Cutting the photocopied pattern as you go along can make cutting the pleated paper easier.

10. When you finish cutting the pattern, carefully unfold the paper to reveal the design.

11. Notice that every other vertical crease contains the cut pattern, while every other vertical crease has not been cut. Carefully accordion pleat the paper by refolding it vertically on each crease so that each crease is folded in the opposite direction than it was originally folded.

12. Repeat steps 4 and 5 with the refolded pleated paper.

13. Take the pleated paper's bottom edge and fold to the 2″ folded edge's crease.

14. Repeat step 13 twice more for a series of folded layers.

15. Repeat step 13 again and unfold, making sure that the fold created a crease in the middle of the pleated paper. The crease divides the pleated paper in half and is the reference point for placing the flowers in the following step.

16. On the *folded* vertical edge, cut flowers above and below the crease created in step 15. Center one three-petal flower in each half of the pleated paper by determining the flower's size and the placement of its top, center, and bottom. Those uncomfortable cutting freestyle can use a pencil to lightly draw half a flower on the pleated paper. Have erasers handy for mistakes. Children can also experiment on small pieces of scrap paper before cutting their paper banners. Flower hand punches and craft punches can also be used. (These professionally made items are available at office supply, drug, stationery, or craft stores in the office supply or photo-album and scrapbook section.) Participants can use their artistic skills in this portion of the craft. Let them vary the size of their flower, make other shapes, and experiment with the cutting materials available.

17. Carefully unfold to reveal the completed pattern.

Note: Papel picado making is usually not so precise unless you are making a design. Have more *papel picado* available so that the children can experiment making random folds and cuts.

PROGRAM AND DISPLAY IDEAS

Depending on your situation and resources, consider having each participant make paper banners for themselves and for your use. It is possible to hang multiple paper banners on strings *(see* below), or hang them individually with tape or pushpins. Hang them at the library's entrances, near the Spanish collection, and on windows and doorways. If you have lots of them, strings of multiple paper banners can be hung from the ceiling in rows or in other eye-catching ways.

The *papel picado* can also be used to decorate another Day of the Dead setting or display. Use them in an *ofrenda* (altar), or have a Day of the Dead *ofrenda*-building program at a later date where they can be used.

Make sure to put up a sign that includes the name and date of the *papel picado* program so that people will know where the banners came from and inquire about future programs.

STRINGING MULTIPLE *PAPEL PICADO* PAPER BANNERS

1. Cut string to desired length. The string has to be long enough to be hung and hold the banners.

2. Place one completed paper banner face-down on a flat surface so that it measures 20″ horizontally.

3. Unfold the 2″ folded edge created in step 2 of the Day of the Dead *Papel Picado* instructions.

4. Place the string along the inside of the folded crease so that the banner can hang from it when it is folded. When working with the first and last banner to be placed

on the string, make sure there is enough string on the end so that the string can be hung.

5. Glue the 2″ folded edge down with the string inside, using a glue stick.

6. Repeat steps 2 to 5, leaving a few inches of string between the individual banners.

7. Let glue dry.

Recommended Books

Amado, Elisa. *Barrilete.*

Anaya, Rudolfo. *Maya's Children.*

Andrade, Mary J. *The Vigil of the Little Angels/La Velación de los Angelitos.*

Anzaldúa, Gloria. *Prietita and the Ghost Woman/Prietita y La Llorona.*

Czernecki, Stefan, and Timothy Rhodes. *The Hummingbird's Gift.*

Hayes, Joe. *La Llorona/The Weeping Woman.*

Krull, Kathleen. *Maria Molina and the Day of the Dead.*

FAMILY PROGRAM
Skeleton Puppet

In Mexican culture, death is not something to be feared and accepted as part of the life cycle; it is traditional to mock death with skeletons during the Day of the Dead. Skeletons are usually doing ordinary things that people do every day, such as playing sports, working, cleaning, and having a good time. Skeleton toys are made of ceramics, wood, and other materials. Here you will make a paper skeleton puppet that can dance everywhere!

Supplies

    white index or card stock paper

    safety scissors

    hole punch

    brass-plated paper fasteners (8 per puppet)

    string

Instructions

1. Copy skeleton pieces onto index or card stock paper.

2. Cut out individual pieces. Cut some beforehand for younger children, or let older family members help cut them. Consider letting the older children cut their own.

3. Use the hole punch to punch holes at the joints and one in the skull so the skeleton can be hung up.

4. Attach pieces with brass-plated paper fasteners at the joints.

Recommended Books

Ancona, George. *Fiesta U.S.A.* (*See* the section on the Day of the Dead.)

Chumba la Cachumba. Illus. Carlos Cotte.

Hayes, Joe. *La Llorona/The Weeping Woman.*

ACTIVITIES

Song

Orozco, José-Luis. "El Día de los Muertos." On *Fiestas/ Holidays: Canciones para Todo el Año.* Arcoiris Records. JL-18 CD Vol. 6. Compact disc.

Poems

Alarcón, Francisco X. "Day of the Dead." In *Angels Ride Bikes and Other Fall Poems/Los Ángeles Andan en Bicicleta y Otros Poemas de Otoño.*

Johnston, Tony. "The Day of the Dead." In *My Mexico/México Mío.*

Soto, Gary. "Ode to La Llorona." In *Neighborhood Odes.*

Essays

Lomas Garza, Carmen. "Dance for the Day of the Dead." In *Magic Windows/Ventanas Mágicas.*

Lomas Garza, Carmen. "The Weeping Woman/La Llorona." In *In My Family/En Mi Familia.*

Drawing by Paul Gonzalez

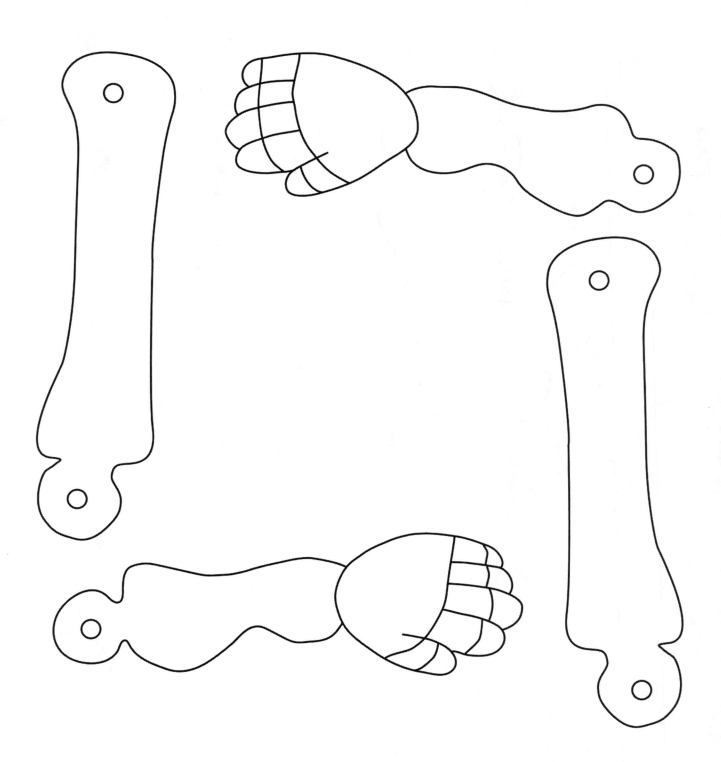

Drawing by Paul Gonzalez

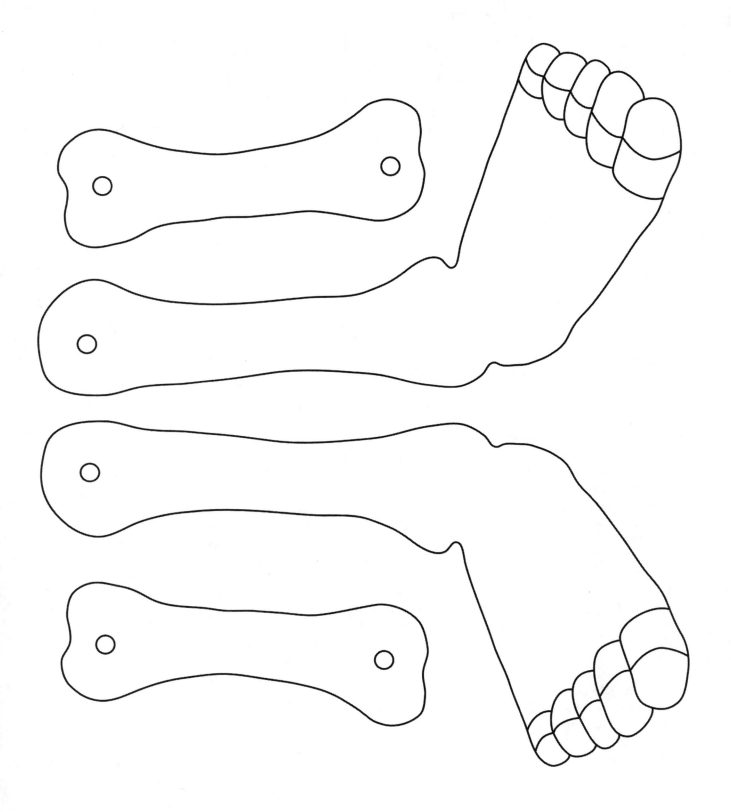

Drawing by Paul Gonzalez

CHAPTER 6

Christmas/ Navidad

In the Latino community, there are many Christmas-related activities during the month of December. These festivities are such a joyous time, they continue into the new year. The Day of Our Lady of Guadalupe is December 12; *Las Posadas*, the reenactment of Mary and Joseph seeking shelter, are December 16 through 24; Christmas Eve is December 24; Christmas is December 25; Three Kings' Day and Epiphany is January 6; and Candlemas is February 2. Each festivity has its own traditions and variations on those traditions, and celebrations vary from country to country, state to state, and city to city.

In Mexico, the holiday season begins with El Día de la Virgen de Guadalupe (or the Day of Our Lady of Guadalupe) on December 12. According to legend, on December 9, 1531, Mary, the mother of Jesus, appeared as a vision to Juan Diego, an Indian, walking on Tepeyac Hill. She told him to tell Bishop Zumárraga, the first bishop of Mexico, to build a church for her on the hill, sacred to the Aztecs. When the bishop did not believe him, Juan Diego returned to the same spot on December 12, and the Virgin Mary miraculously reappeared. She told him to pick a bouquet of roses from the rocky hill, where flowers usually did not grow. Juan Diego put them in his *tilma* (handmade cloak), where the Virgin's image appeared when he attempted to show the roses to the bishop. The Basilica of the Virgin of Guadalupe was built and now houses Juan Diego's *tilma*. Large crowds gather at this church on the hill in Mexico City on December 12, and some make their pilgrimage on their knees.

Las Posadas is a reenactment of Mary and Joseph looking for lodging before the birth of the baby Jesus. The reenactment takes place in neighborhoods from December 16 through 24. Each night of *Las Posadas,* a procession led by those chosen to play Joseph and Mary go to a designated house. Joseph, Mary, and the procession ask for lodging, which the home owner denies through a call and response song. This ritual is repeated at a different house each of the following nights. On the final night of *Las Posadas,* the home owner grants them lodging, the procession enters, and everyone enjoys food, music, and a piñata. In the United States, some of those who continue this tradition reduce the number of *Posada* nights, so hosting a one-night *Posada* celebration is a possibility.

The last night of *Las Posadas* is Christmas Eve. Thus, on December 24, when the participants have been granted lodging, they enjoy the festivities. In many Latin American countries, it is customary to share a special late dinner with family on Christmas Eve. This is an occasion for the country's traditional foods and desserts to be served. Many attend midnight mass, *Misa del Gallo* (literally, "The Rooster's Mass"). At some churches, people line up to offer a gift to the baby Jesus. Because of all this activity, Christmas Day itself is usually pretty quiet. Gifts were traditionally given only on Three Kings' Day (January 6) in many Latino countries, but Christmas gift giving has increased.

Traditionally, Latin American children were unaware of St. Nicholas and Santa Claus because the Three Kings brought them gifts. Upon the birth of the baby Jesus, the Three Kings came from the east to offer him gifts. The details vary, but on the night of January 5, children shine their shoes, write letters to the Three Kings asking for gifts, and gather grass or hay and water for the Three Kings' camels. The next morning, January 6, the children wake up to find their gifts. A parade or a party might occur later in the day. Some prepare a Three Kings' Bread cake shaped like a ring, with a tiny baby doll symbolizing the baby Jesus baked inside, for the day's celebrations. The person who finds the baby doll in his or her piece of cake is obligated to host a party on February 2, Candlemas (or Día de la Candelaria). Candles are blessed on Candlemas, and that day's festivities mark the end of the Christmas season.

PRESCHOOL PROGRAM
Christmas Tree

Children living in Latino countries and Latino children living in the United States now celebrate Christmas with all the symbols familiar to those in the United States—Santa Claus, Christmas trees, and gifts. Preschool-age children enjoy making their own Christmas trees, which make festive holiday decorations for the home or the library.

Supplies

safety scissors

construction, index, or card stock paper (green or white)

crayons or other art supplies

glue sticks

Instructions

1. Photocopy or trace the tree pattern (*see* page 50) and back stand (opposite) onto construction, index, or card stock paper.

2. Cut out the back stand and the tree. Consider doing this before the program or having the children do it.

3. Decorate the tree with crayons or other art supplies.

4. Glue the back stand to the back of the tree so that the tree stands by itself.

Recommended Books

Note: The bibliography at the end of the book provides complete information for each title.

Ada, Alma Flor. *The Christmas Tree/El Árbol de Navidad.*

Jiménez, Francisco. *The Christmas Gift/El Regalo de Navidad.*

Soto, Gary. *Too Many Tamales.*

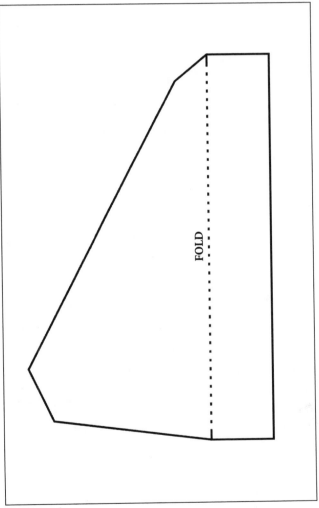

FOLD

Back stand

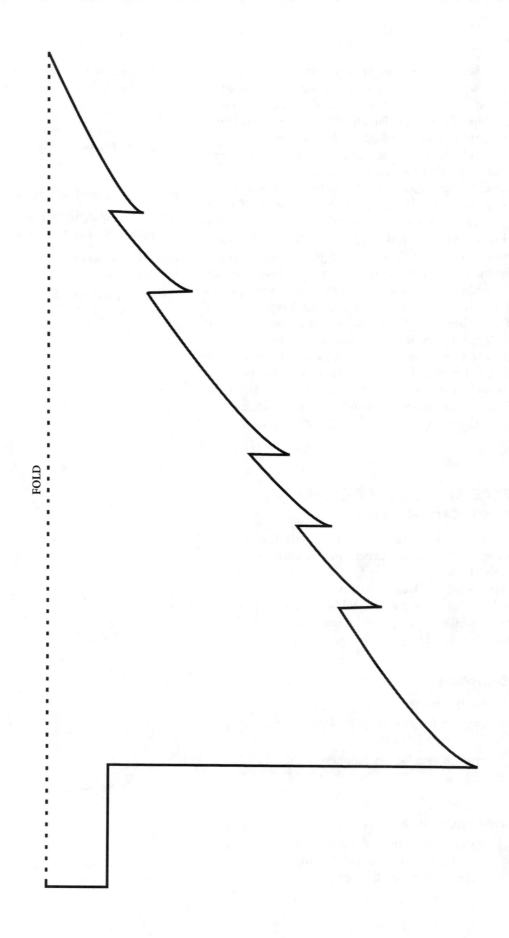

FOLD

PRESCHOOL PROGRAM
Three Kings Silhouettes

Children in Latino countries eagerly await the arrival of the Three Kings, who bring them gifts on Three Kings' Day, or Epiphany, on January 6. Traditions vary, but children prepare by writing letters to the Three Kings asking for gifts, cleaning their shoes, gathering grass or hay, and getting water. The grass or hay may be placed in a shoe, a shoe box, or left near the shoes. The letter may be placed in or near the shoes. All the items may be placed near a door or window where the Three Kings are expected to enter. When the Three Kings arrive, the camels eat the grass or hay and drink the water, and the Three Kings read the letters and leave gifts.

The Bible says that when the baby Jesus was born, three kings, or wise men, came from the east to offer him gifts. Melchior, Gaspar, and Baltazar gave him gifts of gold, frankincense, and myrrh. Here, crafters will make each of the Three Kings offering one of these gifts.

Supplies

safety scissors

white construction, index, or card stock paper

glue sticks

crayons

Instructions

1. Photocopy or trace three back stands (*see* step 1 from the Christmas tree instructions above) and each Three King silhouette onto construction, index, or card stock paper.

2. Cut out the back stands and each silhouette. Consider doing this before the program or having the children do it.

3. Color each silhouette with crayons.

4. Glue one back stand to the back of each Three King silhouette so that each Three King stands by itself.

Recommended Books

Carlson, Lori Marie. *Hurray for Three Kings' Day!*

Mora, Pat. *The Bakery Lady/La Señora de la Panadería.*

Slate, Joseph. *The Secret Stars.*

AFTER-SCHOOL PROGRAM
Ojos de Dios

The Huichol Indians, who live in the Sierra Nevada Mountains near Jalisco, Mexico, almost exclusively created *Ojos de Dios,* or what the first outsider to study the Huichols, Carl Lumholtz, named God's Eyes. The two sticks put together in the shape of the cross represent the four directions—north, south, east, and west—and the four elements—earth, fire, water, and air. Yarn wound around the sticks holds them together. It is customary for the Huichol Indians to give them to newborns for a long life and good health. A few sources say that the center is made at birth and a different color of yarn is added every year until the child's fifth birthday. Most *Ojos de Dios* use sticks approximately 5 inches in length. Folk artists combine several *Ojos de Dios* in different sizes to make one elaborate piece.

Here, use toothpicks to make miniature *Ojos de Dios.* Choose Christmas or other bright colors, and use the *Ojos de Dios* as Christmas tree ornaments, earrings, or pins.

Supplies

round toothpicks

embroidery thread (Christmas or other bright colors)

Instructions

1. Make a cross with two toothpicks.
2. Place the end of the thread near the center of the toothpick cross.

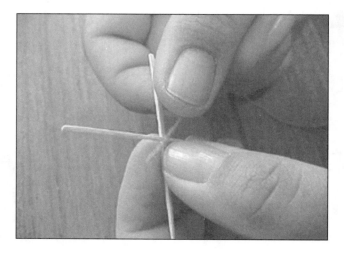

3. The toothpick cross has four quadrants. Join the toothpick cross together by wrapping the thread around two opposite quadrants three times. The tail will be weaved in later, so try to make it as short as possible.

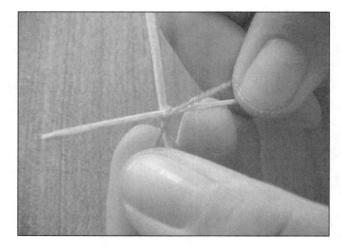

4. Wrap the thread around the other two opposite quadrants three times.

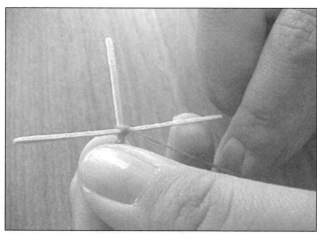

5. Place the thread under one toothpick.
6. Wrap the thread around that toothpick.
7. The thread should now be under the same toothpick. Take the thread and place it under the next toothpick.
8. Make sure that the thread that was wrapped around the previous toothpick is pushed to the cross's center so that it is as close as possible to the thread already on the toothpick.

9. Repeat steps 6 to 8, working on the body of the *Ojo de Dios* in a circular manner (make sure that the tail is weaved in).

10. Stop about ¼" before the outer edge of the toothpick to leave room for the tassels. Leave the remaining thread for use in step 14.

11. Wrap some loose thread twelve times around four fingers and cut to make one tassel batch. Repeat three times, keeping each batch separate.

12. Cut each tassel batch at both ends to make 1¼" strips of thread that are the same length and even on both sides.

13. Lay one tassel batch across one toothpick on the *Ojo de Dios* so that approximately ½" of thread extends beyond the outer edge of the toothpick.

14. Take the thread from the body and wrap it around the tassel batch and toothpick three times to anchor the tassel batch.

15. Pull the other half of the tassel threads toward the outside so that all the tassel thread pieces are in the same position. Continue wrapping the thread from the body around the tassel thread and the toothpick for the desired length. The toothpick must be covered, and the tassel must be anchored. (*See* picture top of page 56.) Thread wrapping anchors the tassel, but it is also decorative as the thread wrapping's width contributes to the project's overall look. Make the four tassels exactly the same or symmetrical with the others.

16. Before moving on to the next toothpick, make sure the bottom of the tassel thread on the toothpick is close to the body so that the toothpick is completely covered with thread. When the toothpick is covered with thread wrapping and the tassel threads look like tassels, continue (make sure not to cut the thread from the body). The thread should be next to the body, so when it moves to the next toothpick, it blends in nicely.

17. Take the thread from the body and take it to the next toothpick in the same manner used to make

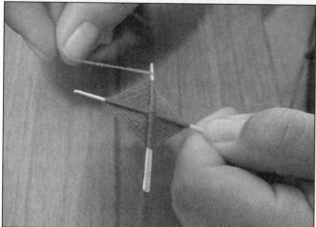

the entire body (steps 5 through 8). Once there, repeat steps 13 through 17 until the tassel on the final toothpick is completed.

18. Upon completion of the final tassel, cut the thread but leave a long tail. Make a loop and pull thread through to knot it. Repeat several times to ensure it doesn't unravel. The string should be cut and tied to form a loop from which the *Ojo de Dios* can be hung.

19. Trim the tassels so that they are the same length.

VARIATIONS

Be creative: Change colors within the body of the *Ojos de Dios* or use more than one color in the tassels.

> *Christmas tree decorations:* Use Christmas or other bright colors to make several *Ojos de Dios* to hang on the Christmas tree.
>
> *Jewelry:* Use 2″ "head pins" and "eye pins," available from a crafts store, to make *Ojo de Dios* earrings and pins, following the steps above. Once the *Ojo de Dios* is finished, use ear wires to make earrings, or attach a 1″ bar pin with a glue gun to make a pin.

Recommended Books

Cruz, Manuel, and Ruth Cruz. *The Chicano Christmas Story.*

Czernecki, Stefan. *Pancho's Piñata.*

Kent, Jack. *The Christmas Piñata.*

Tompert, Ann. *The Silver Whistle.*

FAMILY PROGRAM
Farolitos

Farolitos (small lanterns) and luminarias (paper bags with candles inside) began in New Mexico as little bonfires that were set outside churches. The Chinese began using paper lanterns in the nineteenth century. These lanterns were adapted in New Mexico, where today paper bags with candles inside are used to decorate homes and light the way for *Las Posadas*, the reenactment of Mary and Joseph seeking shelter.

Supplies

brown paper bags (lunch size)

votive candles

sand (can substitute kitty litter) (½ to 1 cup per bag depending on wind currents)

safety scissors

Instructions

1. Lay an unfolded lunch bag on a flat surface so that the unfolded bottom flap touches the flat surface.

2. Fold the unfolded lunch bag in half lengthwise and repeat.

3. Cut shapes on the folded side. Be careful not to cut near the top edge or the bag's bottom.

4. Open up the bag and fold the top edge down 1″. This helps the bag stay open.

5. Pour ½ to 1 cup of sand into the bag, and place the candle in the middle. The sand anchors the candle and the bag, so more weight is needed if the luminaria is placed outdoors in windy weather.

6. Light the candle with a long match.

Recommended Books

Anaya, Rudolfo. *Farolitos for Abuelo.*

Anaya, Rudolfo. *The Farolitos of Christmas.*

Ciavonne, Jean. *Carlos, Light the Farolito.*

Ets, Marie Hall, and Aurora Labastida. *Nine Days to Christmas.*

Hoyt-Goldsmith, Diane. *Las Posadas.*

Politi, Leo. *Pedro, the Angel of Olvera Street.*

Soto, Gary. *Too Many Tamales.*

FAMILY PROGRAM
Poinsettia Paper Flowers

Poinsettias are best known as the Christmas flower and are used for decoration throughout Latin America. The Aztecs named it *cuetlaxochitl*, meaning overblooming flower. It is known as *La Flor de Nochebuena*, the Christmas Eve flower, because though it grows during the months of November, December, and even into January in some places, its leaves turn red most prominently on Christmas Eve. The poinsettia originated in the Mexican states of Guerrero, Chiapas, and Oaxaca. Aztec priests would cultivate it before ceremonies. The Aztecs believed it symbolized new life for their warriors who died in battle. It is called poinsettia after the first U.S. ambassador to Mexico, Joel R. Poinsett, who loved it so, he introduced it to the United States.

This craft is a variation of the paper flowers craft in chapter 7, "Everyday Crafts." Use those instructions.

Instead of using a variety of colored tissue paper, however, use only the color red for all the flowers so that they resemble poinsettias. Use the smaller yellow pieces for the center of each flower.

Recommended Books

DePaola, Tomie. *The Legend of the Poinsettia.*

Mora, Pat, and Charles Ramírez Berg. *The Gift of the Poinsettia/El Regalo de la Flor de Nochebuena.*

Christmas Punch/
Ponche Navideño Recipe

Hot fruit drinks, *ponches*, are very popular during *Las Posadas* (the reenactment of Mary and Joseph seeking shelter) and Christmas festivities. Serve some at your programs during December.

Supplies

1 cup of pitted prunes

1 pound of *tejocotes* (a Mexican fruit) or your favorite fruit if *tejocotes* are hard to find

8 guavas

6 sugarcane sticks, about 3″ long (peeled and cut in half) (found in Mexican or Latino grocery stores; omit this ingredient if desired)

2 cups of dark brown sugar

2 cups of apples (cut into four pieces)

½ cup of raisins

2 oranges (peeled and cut into four pieces)

4 cinnamon sticks (4″ to 6″ long)

2 cups of pears (cut into four pieces)

10 cloves

3 quarts of water

Note: Tejocotes and guavas are somewhat difficult to find, but they can be substituted with the fruit of your choice. Kiwis, pineapple, plums, raisins, or any other fruit will do. This punch can be personalized, so experiment and taste the results.

Instructions

1. Place the water in a large pot.

2. Add the brown sugar, cinnamon sticks, cloves, and sugarcane and bring to a boil.

3. Lower the temperature, add the prunes and *tejocotes*, and cook for about 20 minutes or until the fruit softens.

4. Add the guava, apples, pears, raisins, and oranges, and simmer for 1 hour.

5. Serve the punch hot, being sure to ladle fruit into each mug. More water can be added to the pot if desired.

ACTIVITIES

Song Books

Delacre, Lulu. "Beautiful Bouquet." In *Las Navidades.*

Delacre, Lulu. "The Christmas Season." In *Las Navidades.*

Delacre, Lulu. "The Three Kings." In *Las Navidades.*

Songs

Orozco, José-Luis. "Christmas Bells." On *Diez Deditos—Ten Little Fingers & Other Play Rhymes and Action Songs from Latin America.* Arcoiris Records. JL-22 CD Vol. 12. Compact disc.

Orozco, José-Luis. "Los 3 Reyes." On *Fiestas/Holidays: Canciones para Todo el Año.* Arcoiris Records. JL-18 CD Vol. 6. Compact disc.

Orozco, José-Luis. "Nochebuena/Christmas Eve." On *De Colores and Other Latin-American Folk Songs for Children.* Arcoiris Records. JL-20 CD Vol. 9. Compact disc.

Orozco, José-Luis. "Posadas." On *Fiestas/Holidays: Canciones para Todo el Año.* Arcoiris Records. JL-18 CD Vol. 6. Compact disc.

Poems

Alarcón, Francisco X. "Christmas Eve." In *Iguanas in the Snow and Other Winter Poems/Iguanas en la Nieve y Otros Poemas de Invierno.*

Soto, Gary. "Ode to La Piñata." In *Neighborhood Odes.*

CHAPTER 7

Everyday Crafts

Although many of the previous chapters' crafts have a direct relation to holidays (such as the Day of the Dead *Papel Picado* or the Christmas Three Kings Silhouettes), many crafts can be done at any time. In fact, some crafts are staples of most Latino celebrations. In this chapter, the three crafts—the paper bag piñata, the papier-mâché balloon pinata, and the paper flowers—may be made anytime. Consider having volunteers or staff make them to decorate any programs for the Latino community, or make extras when you have a craft program.

The recipes included here—for *Agua de Jamaica,* Sweet Tamales, and Salsa—can be made and served with any craft program in this book. Likewise, the recommended books and activities in this chapter may be used in any Latino program regardless of when it takes place.

AFTER-SCHOOL PROGRAMS
Piñatas

Traditional piñatas use tissue paper to cover clay pots filled with candy, toys, and other treats. At birthday parties, *Las Posadas* (the reenactment of Mary and Joseph seeking shelter), and other Latino celebrations, children line up to take a turn and try to break the piñata with a stick while blindfolded. When the piñata

is finally broken, its contents fall to the ground, and the children scurry to get them.

The origins of the piñata are uncertain. Some people trace them back to the Aztecs, who celebrated the birthday of Huitzilopóchtli by breaking treat-filled jars at the feet of his statue. Some trace it back to sixteenth-century Italian *pignattas,* similar to the traditional piñata described here.

Today, tissue-covered clay pots, balloons, paper bags, or other containers are used to make piñatas. Piñatas are broken at many children's events in Latin America, and they are more widely sold in the United States because of their increased popularity among non-Latinos. Professionally made piñatas are made into all sorts of shapes, animals, and characters. Here are instructions for a paper bag piñata and for a papier-mâché balloon piñata.

PAPER BAG PIÑATA

Supplies

　　1 lunch bag per piñata

　　safety scissors

　　newspaper

newspaper cut into long strips

2 yards of string per piñata

masking tape

5 pieces of 8½″ × 11″ construction paper per piñata

20 sheets of gift tissue paper per piñata in the piñata's desired bright color (Gift tissue comes in different sizes; any size that measures approximately 20″ × 26″ to 20″ × 29½″ will do.)

engrudo (glue) (*see* the appendix for the recipe—1 batch/4 piñatas)

candy and other treats to fill the piñata (This substantially increases the cost of the craft; you may want to use inexpensive treats or samples or omit.)

Instructions: Piñata Body

1. Stuff the lunch bag with newspaper so that it is firm, and fold the top edge over once.

2. Wrap a 1-yard piece of string twice around the top of the bag, tie it, and fold the bag's edge over once more.

3. Take a 1-yard piece of string, and, on two opposite sides of the bag, tie each end of the string to the string that was wrapped around the bag in step 2 so that the bag can be hung from it.

4. Take one piece of construction paper and roll it up into a cone. Tape it so it does not open.

5. Repeat until you have five cones. The first one determines the size of the cones. Put one inside the other as they are made to ensure equal-sized cones.

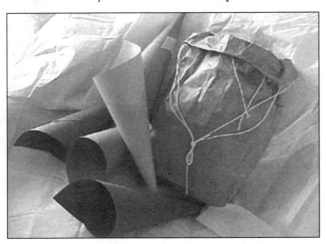

6. On the open end of each cone, cut about 2″ into the cone (vertically toward the pointed end) at 1″ intervals. Bend these pieces outward, so that the cone stands alone.

7. Stuff the cones with newspaper so that they are firm.

8. Tape the cones along the bent pieces to the lunch bag to form a star. Use *engrudo* and newspaper strips to secure the cones to the body and hang. The piñata will hang throughout the following "Decorating Piñata" procedure.

Cones taped to papier-mâchéd bag to form a star. The bottom cone is decorated using Method 2.

Instructions: Decorating Piñata

1. Take one piece of gift tissue paper and fold it full-length accordion style, in 2″ folds lengthwise. Starting on one side, cut lengthwise to produce individual folded strips of tissue paper.

2. Continue by choosing only one of the following methods:

Method 1: Cut fringe on the open edge—cut every inch or so along the open edge. Leave an inch uncut at the top at the folded edge. This creates a shaggy effect. Repeat until you have enough strips to decorate the entire piñata.

Method 2: Cut fringe on folded edge—cut every inch or so along the folded edge. Leave an inch at the top at the open edge. Turn the tissue paper strip inside out so that the folded uncut edge becomes the fringe. This creates a curly effect. Repeat until you have enough strips to decorate the entire piñata.

3. Hang the piñata somewhere where it can turn on its own.

4. Spread a thin layer of *engrudo* on the cone that you will work on.

5. Starting at the pointed tip, wrap tissue paper strips around the cone until the entire cone is covered.

6. Wrap tissue paper strips around all the cones before you do the body.

7. Wrap tissue paper strips around the body. Here, the body is decorated using Method 1, and the cones are decorated using Method 2. When the body is completely covered, make the tassels.

Instructions: Tassels

1. Take one piece of gift tissue paper and fold it full-length accordion style, in 2″ folds lengthwise.

2. Fold in half.

3. Cut lengthwise evenly about five times leaving about an inch at the top of the folded side.

4. Open and cut into 6″ pieces. Cut on the accordion folds.

5. Take four pieces, roll together at the top, and pinch tight when finished. Tape if desired.

6. Cut tip of cone enough to insert pinched tip and tassel.

7. Twist until secure.

8. Repeat with each cone.

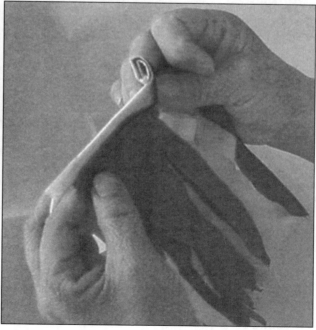

9. Once the piñata is dry, pull out some of the newspaper from the opening at the top of the pinata, and fill the completed piñata with candy and other treats.

PAPIER-MÂCHÉ BALLOON PIÑATA

Supplies

same as "Paper Bag Piñata" above

size 11 round balloon

Instructions

1. Blow up round balloon.

2. Cut newspaper into 2″ × 2″ square pieces.

3. Use *engrudo* to paste newspaper to the balloon until it is completely covered with two layers.

4. Let it dry overnight.

5. Once it is dry, pop the balloon. Take it out or leave it there. Make an opening at the top to put in candy.

6. Make two holes on either side to put string that will hang the piñata.

7. Continue by following instructions for "Paper Bag Piñata," starting with step 3 listed under "Piñata Body."

Recommended Books

Note: The bibliography at the end of the book provides complete information for each title.

Ancona, George. *The Piñata Maker/El Piñatero.*

Czernecki, Stefan, and Timothy Rhodes. *Pancho's Piñata.*

Ets, Marie Hall, and Aurora Labastida. *Nine Days to Christmas.*

Guy, Ginger Foglesong. *¡Fiesta!*

Kent, Jack. *The Christmas Piñata.*

Kleven, Elisa. *Hooray, a Piñata!*

Lomas Garza, Carmen. "Birthday Party/Cumpleaños." In *Family Pictures/Cuadros de Familia.*

FAMILY PROGRAM
Paper Flowers

Flowers are very popular decorations throughout the world and Latin America. In Mexico, flowers are used as motifs on folk art, such as tin art, or made out of other materials, such as corn husks or tissue paper. Tissue paper came to Mexico from China in the seventeenth or eighteenth century and was very inexpensive, making it readily available to people of all economic backgrounds. Today, tissue paper is still used in many Mexican crafts, including the world-renowned Mexican paper flowers. These colorful flowers decorate homes, hotels, churches, and every other place imaginable.

Supplies

tissue paper (bright colors)

yellow tissue paper

flower stem wire (18 gauge; length, 18″)

flower stem tape (in desired color)

safety scissors

Instructions

1. Cut a standard sheet of gift tissue paper in half so that it measures 10″ x 13″. Cut five pieces in the desired color of the flower.

2. Cut a smaller piece of yellow tissue paper so that it measures 3″ × 10″.

3. Pile the five pieces of tissue paper and place the smaller yellow piece of paper in their center.

4. Fold it accordion style—using about 1″ folds.

5. Fold it in half.

6. Place the stem wire in the middle, and twist the wire along the stem.

7. Wrap flower stem tape around the wire until it reaches the bottom.

8. Cut the folded tip on the end of the tissue paper, at an angle if desired. Trimming the edges determines the flower's flare.

9. Open up the tissue on either side.

10. Pull layers of tissue paper out one by one, giving the flower shape.

Note: The size of the flower is determined by the size of the paper, so you can make flowers larger or smaller. The wire determines the length of the stem.

Recommended Books

Cherry, Lynne, and Mark J. Plotkin. *The Shaman's Apprentice.*

Delacre, Lulu. *Arroz con Leche.*

Griego, Margot C., and Betsy L. Bucks. *Tortillas para Mamá and Other Nursery Rhymes/Spanish and English.*

Mora, Pat. *Delicious Hullabaloo/Pachanga Deliciosa.*

Rohmer, Harriet. *Uncle Nacho's Hat/El Sombrero del Tío Nacho.*

Señor Cat's Romance and Other Favorite Stories from Latin America. Retold by Lucía M. González.

Soto, Gary. *Snapshots from the Wedding.*

AGUA DE JAMAICA (HIBISCUS FLOWER-FLAVORED WATER) RECIPE

Aguas are flavored waters made out of seeds, powder, or fruit. Unlike juices, *aguas* are relatively clear as they are a combination of water and the main ingredient. The type of flavored drink determines how difficult it is to make. Mexican markets, delis, and restaurants sell them, but you can make your own.

The following is a simple recipe using hibiscus flowers. Serve it at your events. It's very tasty and known to be good for the digestion.

Ingredients

2 cups of dried hibiscus flowers (available at herb, health-food, Mexican, or Asian markets)

4 cups of water

2½ cups of sugar

Instructions

1. Bring to a boil 4 cups of water in a large saucepan.

2. Carefully add the hibiscus flowers to the boiling water and simmer for about 3 minutes.

3. Remove the saucepan from the stove, and let the brew cool to room temperature.

4. Strain the liquid into a pitcher.

5. Add the sugar and enough water to make a gallon.

6. Serve over ice.

SWEET TAMALES RECIPE

Tamales are made a little differently in each country, state, region, city or town, and home. Making tamales usually involves the entire family, where everyone contributes to making dozens of tamales at a time. Many Latin American countries serve tamales on Christmas Eve, but they are eaten year-round. Because they are made in such large quantities, they are an ideal choice for large celebrations. Most tamales are filled with meat or some sort of vegetable. A sweet tamale is made by adding sugar and other sweet items to the *masa* (dough). For your program, ask a restaurant to donate tamales or a community member to make some homemade ones. If you decide to make your own, try this delicious version of a sweet tamale recipe.

Ingredients

60 corn husks (Corn husks can be purchased in Latino grocery stores or in the "spices" or "Hispanic" sections of supermarkets.)

2 cups of brown or white sugar

5 pounds of prepared *masa* (dough) (found in Latino markets and delis)

1 quart of water

1 cup of raisins (optional—vary amount as desired)

14-oz. can of pineapple chunks (optional—drain the juice and cut into smaller pieces)

Note: Makes approximately five dozen tamales.

Instructions

1. Mix sugar (and raisins and/or pineapples) into the *masa* with your hands.

2. Soak corn husks in warm water for flexibility (approximately 30 minutes). Remove the corn strings so that the husks are clean.

3. Shake water off of the corn husks. Pat dry or drain.

4. Take a corn husk leaf and determine which is the inside and the outside. The inside is softer than the outside.

5. Take a heaping tablespoon of *masa* and place it in the middle of the inside of the corn husk. Fold the corn husk vertically, and then fold the corn husk horizontally from one end only.

6. Take a little piece of corn husk and tie the two ends together. When making large quantities of different kinds of tamales, wrapping them differently helps identify them after they are cooked.

7. Tamales need to be steamed. Put them in a *tamalera,* a pot specifically designed to cook tamales, or in a large saucepan with a vegetable steamer. Stack them vertically leaning toward the center with the tied end facing up. Placing a vegetable steamer upside down will make this easier. If you are cooking meat and sweet tamales together in the same steamer, put the sweet ones on top.

8. Cover the tamales with an additional layer of corn husk leaves.

9. Place a clean wet cloth over the leaves and pour in a quart of water.

10. Put on high heat until the water boils. Then turn the heat down to medium, and cook for 50 minutes.

11. Test one by removing the corn husk. If the corn husk comes off easily and the tamale is solid, the tamales are ready.

SALSA RECIPE

Salsa has many roles, and it would be hard to find a table with Latino food where it is not present. It is served with tortilla chips, on top of traditional main dishes such as flautas and *carne asada* (steak), and as one of many ingredients in such dishes as burritos and *gorditas* (thick tortillas filled with all sorts of ingredients; *see* chapter 3 for a *gorditas* family program). Salsa can be mild or spicy depending on its ingredients. As with many Latino recipes, there are as many variations as there are cooks!

Ingredients

2 jalapeño chiles

2 tomatoes (red)

½ onion

2 or 3 cloves of garlic

2 cups of water

½ teaspoon of salt

Instructions

1. Wash the chiles and tomatoes, and peel the cloves of garlic.
2. Place all of the ingredients except the salt into a saucepan with the water and bring to a boil.
3. Let the ingredients cool until you can handle them with your hands.
4. Once cooled, remove the stems from the chiles and tomatoes.
5. Drain all but 2 cups of the water from the saucepan.
6. Place all of the ingredients in the blender, add the salt, and chop.

Note: This recipe makes approximately 2 cups of salsa. Canned tomato sauce can be added to the mixture if the salsa is too spicy.

ACTIVITIES

Song Books

Delacre, Lulu. "Beautiful Bouquet." In *Las Navidades.*

Delacre, Lulu. "The Christmas Season." In *Las Navidades.*

Delacre, Lulu. "The Three Kings." In *Las Navidades.*

Songs

Orozco, José-Luis. "Christmas Bells." On *Diez Deditos—Ten Little Fingers & Other Play Rhymes and Action Songs from Latin America.* Arcoiris Records. JL-22 CD Vol. 12. Compact disc.

Orozco, José-Luis. "Los 3 Reyes." On *Fiestas/Holidays: Canciones para Todo el Año.* Arcoiris Records. JL-18 CD Vol. 6. Compact disc.

Orozco, José-Luis. "Nochebuena/Christmas Eve." On *De Colores and Other Latin-American Folk Songs for Children.* Arcoiris Records. JL-20 CD Vol. 9. Compact disc.

Orozco, José-Luis. "Posadas." On *Fiestas/Holidays: Canciones para Todo el Año.* Arcoiris Records. JL-18 CD Vol. 6. Compact disc.

Poems

Alarcón, Francisco X. "Christmas Eve." In *Iguanas in the Snow and Other Winter Poems/Iguanas en la Nieve y Otros Poemas de Invierno.*

Soto, Gary. "Ode to La Piñata." In *Neighborhood Odes.*

Essay

Lomas Garza, Carmen. "Birthday Party." In *Family Pictures/Cuadros de Familia.*

| APPENDIX

Engrudo and Migajón

ENGRUDO/GLUE RECIPE

This *engrudo*/glue is used throughout Mexico in papier-mâché and piñata making. The ingredients are common and inexpensive, making them available to people of all economic classes.

Ingredients

1 cup of water
½ cup of flour

Instructions

1. Heat water.
2. When it is a little warm, slowly add flour while stirring to prevent lumps.
3. Lower heat and cook for 5 minutes, stirring constantly.

Note: This makes about ¾ of a cup.

MIGAJÓN/DOUGH RECIPE

Migajón is a bread dough used to make various crafts. The ingredients are easily obtainable and inexpensive, and *migajón*-based crafts are common throughout Mexico.

Ingredients

3 slices of white bread (Wonder Bread works best)
3 tablespoons of white glue (Elmer's works best)

Instructions

1. Remove crusts from the bread.
2. Shred the bread into a bowl.
3. Add glue and knead with wooden spoon.
4. Knead it until it is smooth.
5. To make larger portions, add 1 tablespoon of glue for each slice of bread.
6. If the dough is too sticky, add bread; if the dough is too dry, add glue.
7. It will keep for several weeks but must be sealed in a plastic bag and refrigerated.
8. Mix with acrylic paint or food coloring to color if desired.

Suggestions: Use *migajón* to make figurines. Make a hole at the top of the figurine to run yarn through, and hang the items. Be sure to let the items dry for several days before hanging them. When making *migajón* crafts, provide small pieces of cardboard, or ask participants to bring their own. The children can take their crafts home on the cardboard while they wait for them to dry. Or take advantage if you have hanging space and display the crafts in the library.

Bibliography

Ada, Alma Flor. *The Christmas Tree/El Árbol de Navidad: A Christmas Rhyme in English and Spanish.* Illus. Terry Ybáñez. New York: Hyperion, 1997.

In this cumulative tale, each family member adds a Christmas ornament to the tree.

Ada, Alma Flor. *Gathering the Sun: An Alphabet in Spanish and English.* Illus. Simón Silva. New York: Lothrop, Lee & Shepard, 1997.

Through a bilingual poem for each letter of the alphabet, this tribute to migrant life, accompanied by full-page artwork, is appropriate for all ages.

Ada, Alma Flor. *The Lizard and the Sun: An Old Mexican Folk-Tale.* Illus. Felipe Dávalos. Trans. Rosalma Zubizarreta. New York: Doubleday, 1997.

The sun has disappeared, and all the animals stop searching for him except for the lizard, who finally finds him. The finest dancers and musicians perform in front of the highest pyramid until the sun rises. This becomes an annual feast so that the sun will not disappear again.

Ada, Alma Flor, and F. Isabel Campoy. *Paths.* Miami: Santillana USA Publishing Company, 2000.

One of a four-part biography series, this installment includes short biographies on Rita Moreno, Fernando Botero, and Evelyn Cisneros. Paintings and photographs accompany the informative and simple text, sure to appeal to all ages. This book is also available in Spanish under the title *Pasos.*

Ada, Alma Flor, and F. Isabel Campoy. *Smiles.* Miami: Santillana USA Publishing Company, 2000.

One of a four-part biography series, this installment includes short biographies on Pablo Picasso, Gabriela Mistral, and Benito Juárez. Paintings and photographs accompany the informative and simple text, sure to appeal to all ages. This title is also available in Spanish under the title *Sonrisas.*

Ada, Alma Flor, and F. Isabel Campoy. *Steps.* Miami: Santillana USA Publishing Company, 2000.

One of a four-part biography series, this installment includes short biographies on José Martí, Frida Kahlo, and César Chávez. Paintings and photographs accompany the informative and simple text, sure to appeal to all ages. This book is also available in Spanish under the title *Caminos.*

Ada, Alma Flor, and F. Isabel Campoy. *Voices.* Miami: Santillana USA Publishing Company, 2000.

One of a four-part biography series, this installment includes short biographies on Luis Valdez, Judith F. Baca, and Carlos J. Finley. Paintings and photographs accompany the informative and simple text, sure to appeal to all ages. This book is also available in Spanish under the title *Voces.*

Alarcón, Francisco X. *Angels Ride Bikes and Other Fall Poems/Los Ángeles Andan en Bicicleta y Otros Poemas de Otoño.* Illus. Maya Christina Gonzalez. San Francisco: Children's Book Press, 1999.

The fall entry of this poetry series covering the different seasons, this volume focuses on the poet's family and their move to Los Angeles.

Alarcón, Francisco X. *From the Bellybutton of the Moon and Other Summer Poems/Del Ombligo de la Luna y Otros Poemas de Verano.* Illus. Maya Christina

Gonzalez. San Francisco: Children's Book Press, 1998.

Part of a four-part series, this poetry collection covers summertime activities and events.

Alarcón, Francisco X. *Iguanas in the Snow and Other Winter Poems/Iguanas en la Nieve y Otros Poemas de Invierno*. Illus. Maya Christina Gonzalez. San Francisco: Children's Book Press, 2001.

Winter is celebrated in San Francisco and the Sierra Nevada in this final installment of seasonal poetry.

Alarcón, Francisco X. *Laughing Tomatoes and Other Spring Poems/Jitomates Risueños y Otros Poemas de Primavera*. Illus. Maya Christina Gonzalez. San Francisco: Children's Book Press, 1998.

The first of this successful series of seasonal poetry collections by the award-winning poet and illustrator team, the bright-colored visuals and poems make poetry fun for children. Spring is the focus of this volume.

Alvarez, Julia. *The Secret Footprints*. New York: Knopf, 2000.

This Dominican folktale features the legendary *ciguapa*, a tribe of beautiful underwater people. Guapa, a brave, bold young girl, is curious about humans. One day she finally makes contact, against her people's wishes, and discovers human kindness before her people sneak her away.

Amado, Elisa. *Barrilete: A Kite for the Day of the Dead*. Toronto: Groundwood Books, 1999.

In Santiago Sacatepéquez, Guatemala, the village people prepare giant kites for the Day of the Dead. This photo-essay follows Juan through all the preparations for celebrating this famous annual event and flying the kite.

Anaya, Rudolfo. *Farolitos for Abuelo*. Illus. Edward Gonzales. New York: Hyperion, 1998.

In this sequel to *The Farolitos of Christmas*, Luz has a special relationship with her grandfather. Unfortunately, he catches pneumonia after he saves a child who falls in the river, and he dies. Luz misses her grandfather and remembers him by tending his garden. When Christmas comes, she takes *farolitos*, small lanterns, to his grave. Others join her, and a new tradition begins.

Anaya, Rudolfo. *The Farolitos of Christmas*. Illus. Edward Gonzales. New York: Hyperion, 1995.

In a New Mexico village, Luz worries that her family won't be able to create the traditional luminarias, small bonfires of stacked wood, on Christmas Eve because her father is fighting in World War II and her grandfather is sick. They decide to make *farolitos*, small lanterns, instead, using paper bags, sand, and candles.

Anaya, Rudolfo. *Maya's Children: The Story of La Llorona*. Illus. Maria Baca. New York: Hyperion, 1997.

In this version of La Llorona, the wailing woman searching for her children, Maya is destined to live forever. The animals tell Maya how to keep her beautiful children safe. But Señor Tiempo (Time) is determined to make sure that her children do not live forever and sets out to deceive her.

Ancona, George. *Barrio: José's Neighborhood*. New York: Harcourt, 1998.

This photo-essay centers on José, who lives in San Francisco's Mission District, where he enjoys Latino celebrations and traditions with his family and community.

Ancona, George. *Fiesta U.S.A.* New York: Lodestar, 1995.

This book contains photo-essays on different Latino holiday celebrations in different parts of the United States.

Ancona, George. *Pablo Remembers: The Fiesta of the Day of the Dead*. New York: Lothrop, Lee & Shepard, 1993.

During the Day of the Dead celebration, a young Mexican boy and his family make elaborate preparations to honor the spirits of the dead. Includes activities at the market, home, church, and cemetery.

Ancona, George. *The Piñata Maker/El Piñatero*. San Diego, Calif.: Harcourt, 1995.

This bilingual photo-essay in English and Spanish follows a seventy-seven-year-old piñata maker in southern Mexico known as Tío Rico. The photographs illustrate how he makes all sorts of piñatas and life-size puppets. Because he is invited to all the parties, we see a piñata broken at a birthday party, and boys dance in the life-size puppets he made.

Andrade, Mary J. *The Vigil of the Little Angels: Day of the Dead in Mexico/La Velación de los Angelitos: Día de Muertos en México.* Illus. José J. Murguía. San Jose, Calif.: La Oferta Review, 2001.

The author of books on this topic for adults has written this children's book using her photos and the illustrator's paintings to focus on the traditions on Janitzio Island, Michoacán, Mexico.

Anzaldúa, Gloria. *Prietita and the Ghost Woman/ Prietita y La Llorona.* Illus. Maya Christina Gonzalez. San Francisco: Children's Book Press, 1996.

When Prietita gets lost trying to find the plant the healer needs to heal her mother, she bumps into La Llorona, the traditional folk character used to scare children. Here, La Llorona plays a different role and teaches us that things aren't always as they seem.

Argueta, Jorge. *A Movie in My Pillow/Una Película en Mi Almohada.* Illus. Elizabeth Gómez. San Francisco: Children's Book Press, 2001.

This poetry collection is a memoir of when the poet came to the United States from El Salvador as a boy because of El Salvador's civil war in 1980. Beautifully illustrated, the poems reflect on his life in El Salvador and in his Latino neighborhood in the United States and on things of importance to children.

Behrens, June. *¡Fiesta! Cinco de Mayo.* Chicago: Children's Press, 1978.

This photo-essay for children illustrates Cinco de Mayo festivities. Although the text briefly describes the history, most of the book describes the activities depicted in park and school celebrations. Intended for primary elementary school students.

Brock, Virginia. *Piñatas.* Nashville, Tenn.: Abingdon, 1966.

This book offers background information on piñatas and three piñata stories as well as instructions on how to make and use a piñata. Twelve individual piñatas are featured, including a birthday cake, clown, football, and star.

Carlson, Lori Marie. *Hurray for Three Kings' Day!* Illus. Ed Martinez. New York: Morrow Junior Books, 1999.

In an effort to be inclusive, the author combines different Three Kings' Day traditions in this story focusing on Anita and her family. The night before Three Kings' Day, exhausted from that night's activities, Anita puts out gifts for the Three Kings. The next morning everyone opens gifts. The day's celebration ends with the Three Kings' Bread cake.

Carlson, Lori Marie, ed. *Sol a Sol: Bilingual Poems Written and Selected by Lori Marie Carlson.* Illus. Emily Lisker. New York: Holt, 1998.

Illustrated bilingual poems in picture-book format.

Carmichael, Elizabeth. *The Skeleton at the Feast: The Day of the Dead in Mexico.* Austin: University of Texas Press, 1992.

This is a very detailed look at the Day of the Dead in Mexico filled with sketches, black-and-white and color photographs, and personal interviews. An excellent resource.

Casteneda, Omar S. *Abuela's Weave.* Illus. Enrique O. Sanchez. New York: Lee & Low, 1993.

Esperanza and her grandmother work hard to weave traditional Guatemalan tapestries and *huipiles* (blouses). When they finally have enough to sell, they travel separately to the market, where Esperanza is intimidated by the works of others.

Chavarría-Cháirez, Becky. *Magda's Tortillas/Las Tortillas de Magda.* Illus. Anne Vega. Houston: Piñata Books, 2000.

Magda is finally old enough to learn how to make tortillas. Unfortunately, her tortillas are not perfectly round like her grandmother's but come out in different shapes, such as hearts, stars, and even a hexagon.

Cherry, Lynne, and Mark J. Plotkin. *The Shaman's Apprentice: A Tale of the Amazon Rain Forest.* New York: Voyager Books, 2001.

When an outsider informs those in an Indian village deep in the Amazon rain forest that their medicinal plants cure disease, a young man who has followed the shaman (the medicine man who saved his life) becomes his apprentice.

Chumba la Cachumba. Illus. Carlos Cotte. Caracas, Venezuela: Edíciones Ekaré, 1995.

This traditional song is put into a picture-book format depicting skeleton activity.

Ciavonne, Jean. *Carlos, Light the Farolito.* Illus. Donna Clair. New York: Clarion, 1995.

Carlos has to take his grandfather's role in *Las Posadas,* the reenactment of Mary and Joseph seeking shelter, when he is late.

Cisneros, Sandra. *Hair/Pelitos.* Illus. Terry Ybáñez. Trans. Liliana Valenzuela. New York: Apple Soup, 1994.

A picture-book adaptation of a vignette from Cisneros's *The House on Mango Street* that describes how everyone in Esmeralda's family has different hair.

Corpi, Lucha. *Where Fireflies Dance/Ahí Donde Bailan las Luciérnagas.* San Francisco: Children's Book Press, 1997.

A girl and her brother sneak into a haunted house where Mexican revolutionary Juan Sebastián once lived. After the children are caught, their grandmother tells the story about Juan Sebastián fulfilling his destiny. This inspires the girl to find her own destiny.

Cruces Carvajal, Ramón. *Lo Que México Aportó al Mundo.* Mexico D.F.: Panorama Editorial, 1986.

This book is a resource for what Mexico gave the world.

Cruz, Manuel, and Ruth Cruz. *The Chicano Christmas Story.* Pasadena, Calif.: Bilingual Educational Services, 1980.

This picture book tells the story of a Latino family moving from place to place to find work. Right before Christmas, there is no work, and they have no gifts to offer. In addition, the son in the story has not heard of Santa Claus because he is used to Mexican custom and wonders why Santa has never visited him.

Czernecki, Stefan, and Timothy Rhodes. *The Hummingbird's Gift.* Illus. Juliana Reyes de Silva and Juan Hilario Silva. New York: Hyperion, 1994.

The Day of the Dead and straw weavings, called *panicuas,* are featured in this telling of the Tzintzuntzan Mexican village legend. This picture book is beautifully illustrated not only with colorful paintings, but with creative use of straw weavings on the pages with text.

Czernecki, Stefan, and Timothy Rhodes. *Pancho's Piñata.* Illus. Stefan Czernecki. New York: Hyperion, 1992.

A star gets stuck on a cactus when he attempts to get closer to Pancho, the little boy leading Las Posadas (the reenactment of Mary and Joseph seeking shelter), with his angelic singing. Stardust falls on Pancho when he sets the star free. Pancho thanks the star for his gift of happiness every night of his life. When he is old, Pancho makes a piñata that gives gifts to everyone.

Delacre, Lulu. *Arroz con Leche: Popular Songs and Rhymes from Latin America.* New York: Scholastic, 1984.

Traditional illustrated songs from throughout Latin America in English and Spanish. Brief background text accompanies the songs when appropriate. Music also included.

Delacre, Lulu. *Las Navidades: Popular Christmas Songs from Latin America.* New York: Scholastic, 1990.

Illustrated Christmas songs from throughout Latin America in English and Spanish. Brief background text accompanies each song. Music also included.

DePaola, Tomie. *The Legend of the Poinsettia.* New York: Putnam, 1994.

Lucida's mother gets sick before Christmas. They had been working on a blanket to give the baby Jesus, but Lucida is too little to finish it alone. On the way to church, she meets an elderly woman who reassures her that her mother will recover and that any gift she gives the baby Jesus will be loved because it came from her. Lucida gathers weeds, offers them to the baby Jesus, and prays; and the weeds miraculously turn into poinsettias, as do all the green weeds growing outside.

Dorros, Arthur. *Abuela.* Illus. Elisa Kleven. New York: Dutton, 1991.

In this picture book, Rosalba and her grandmother fly through New York City.

Dorros, Arthur. *Isla.* Illus. Elisa Kleven. New York: Dutton, 1991.

In this sequel to *Abuela,* Rosalba and her grandmother fly to Puerto Rico.

Downs, Cynthia, and Terry Becker. *Bienvenidos: A Monthly Bilingual/Bicultural Teacher's Resource Guide to Mexico & Hispanic Culture.* Illus. Margherita DePaulis. Minneapolis, Minn.: T. S. Denison and Company, 1991.

This very complete resource for teachers includes history, crafts, songs, and activities.

The Eagle on the Cactus: Traditional Stories from Mexico. Retold by Angel Vigil. Englewood, Colo.: Libraries Unlimited, 2000.

The book contains legends, creation stories, trickster tales, other folktales, and background information.

Ehlert, Lois. *Moon Rope: A Peruvian Folktale/Un Lazo a la Luna: Una Leyenda Peruana.* New York: Harcourt Brace & Company, 1992.

Fox and Mole attempt to climb to the moon in this bilingual picture book. When Mole slips climbing the rope, he is so embarrassed he comes out only at night and never listens to a fox. Did Fox make it? The birds say they can see Fox on a full moon.

Elya, Susan Middleton. *Say Hola to Spanish.* Illus. Loretta Lopez. New York: Lee & Low, 1996.

This rhyming picture book introduces readers to Spanish by inserting Spanish words within the English text. The Spanish words are used in context and aided by visuals, which helps listeners decipher their meaning.

Ets, Marie Hall, and Aurora Labastida. *Nine Days to Christmas.* New York: Viking, 1959.

This Caldecott Medal–winning book tells the story of a little Mexican girl who is finally old enough to have a *Posada* (the reenactment of Mary and Joseph seeking shelter). Choosing her own piñata adds to her excitement.

García, Richard. *My Aunt Otilia's Spirits/Los Espíritus de Mi Tía Otilia.* San Francisco: Children's Book Press, 1987.

When Aunt Otilia comes to visit, her nephew cannot sleep because of the knocks on the wall and the shaking of the bed. She explains that the commotion is just her spirits and that he should go to sleep. One night he stays awake, and Aunt Otilia may never be the same . . .

Geeslin, Campbell. *How Nanita Learned to Make Flan.* Illus. Petra Mathers. New York: Atheneum Books for Young Readers, 1999.

Because her papa is so busy making shoes for all the townspeople, Nanita has no shoes. She decides to make herself a pair of shoes and wears them to bed one night. They cause her to sleepwalk, and she awakens in the desert outside a grand house where the ranchero and an old woman force her to do chores and make a delicious flan. This story also contains the recipe for Nanita's flan.

Gollub, Matthew. *The Moon Was at a Fiesta.* Illus. Leovigildo Martinez. Santa Rosa, Calif.: Tortuga Press, 1997.

This tale explains why Oaxacans say "the moon was at a fiesta" when the moon stays up past dawn. Jealous that all the parties were held when the sun shined, the moon decides to hold a party when it shines. The book illustrates preparing for a fiesta with Latino food and decorations.

Gollub, Matthew. *The Twenty-Five Mixtec Cats.* Illus. Leovigildo Martinez. New York: Tambourine Books, 1993.

Basing the tale on Oaxacan folklore, Gollub tells of the *curandero* (healer) who returned from a Mixtec market with twenty-five cats. Everyone in the village feared the cats. As the cats grew, they learned how to help the *curandero,* and the villagers sought out an evil *curandero* to rid the village of the cats. Their plan backfires, and the cats eventually save the day.

Griego, Margot C., and Betsy L. Bucks. Select. and trans. Sharon S. Gilbert and Laurel H. Kimball. *Tortillas para Mamá and Other Nursery Rhymes/*

Spanish and English. Illus. Barbara Cooney. New York: Holt, 1981.

Traditional Spanish rhymes and finger plays are translated into English and illustrated in this picture book.

Guy, Ginger Foglesong. *¡Fiesta!* Illus. Rene King Moreno. New York: Greenwillow Books, 1996.

Children prepare for a party in this bilingual counting book.

Harris, Zoe, and Suzanne Williams. *Piñatas & Smiling Skeletons: Celebrating Mexican Festivals.* Illus. Yolanda Garfias Woo. Berkeley, Calif.: Pacific View Press, 1998.

Covers Mexican celebrations such as the Festival of Guadalupe, Christmas, Carnaval, Corpus Christi, Independence Day, and Day of the Dead. Descriptions include celebrations in different parts of Mexico and in the United States. Includes crafts, recipes, and legends.

Hayes, Joe. *¡El Cucuy! A Bogeyman Cuento in English and Spanish.* Illus. Honorio Robledo. El Paso, Tex.: Cinco Puntos Press, 2001.

Parents warn their children that the legendary Cucuy will take them away if they misbehave. In this story, El Cucuy takes away two girls because they treat their little sister poorly.

Hayes, Joe. *La Llorona/The Weeping Woman: An Hispanic Legend Told in Spanish and English.* Illus. Vicki Trego Hill. El Paso, Tex.: Cinco Puntos Press, 1987.

In this cautionary folktale widely known throughout Mexico and the southwestern United States, a heartbroken mother throws her children in the river and drowns searching for them. Legend has it that she can still be heard near rivers searching for her children, so all children should avoid being captured by her!

Herrera, Juan Felipe. *Laughing Out Loud, I Fly: Poems in English and Spanish.* Illus. Karen Barbour. New York: HarperCollins, 1998.

Poetry anthology for older elementary school children.

Hopkins, Jackie Mims. *The Horned Toad Prince.* Illus. Michael Austin. Atlanta: Peachtree Publishers, 2000.

This southwestern version of the *Frog Prince* contains a sprinkling of Spanish words throughout the text and a surprise ending.

Hoyt-Goldsmith, Diane. *Day of the Dead: A Mexican-American Celebration.* Illus. Lawrence Migdale. New York: Holiday House, 1994.

Day of the Dead celebrations in Sacramento, California, are seen through the eyes of ten-year-old twins. Though including history and explaining different elements, the events are personalized through the family and community traditions shared in the text and accompanying photographs. Also includes a mask-making technique using plaster-casting materials.

Hoyt-Goldsmith, Diane. *Las Posadas: An Hispanic Christmas Celebration.* New York: Holiday House, 1999.

This photo-essay follows eleven-year-old Kristen and *Las Posadas* festivities, the reenactment of Mary and Joseph seeking shelter, in Española, New Mexico. The text includes history on *Las Posadas,* craft making, cooking, luminarias, *farolitos* (small lanterns), and other traditions. Includes Spanish and English lyrics and music for "The Song of *Las Posadas"* and recipe for *biscochitos* (cookies).

Jaffe, Nina. *The Golden Flower: A Taino Myth from Puerto Rico.* Illus. Enrique O. Sánchez. New York: Simon & Schuster, 1996.

This book illustrates how the island of Puerto Rico came to be.

Jiménez, Francisco. *The Christmas Gift/El Regalo de Navidad.* Illus. Claire B. Cotts. Boston: Houghton Mifflin, 2000.

A young boy worries he will not receive his Christmas gift because his migrant family moves right before Christmas.

Jiménez, Francisco. *The Circuit: Stories for the Life of a Migrant Child.* Albuquerque: University of New Mexico Press, 1997.

Short stories about a migrant child growing up in California.

Johnston, Tony. *Day of the Dead.* Illus. Jeanette Winter. New York: Harcourt, 1997.

This beautifully illustrated picture book depicts preparations for the Day of the Dead celebration: creating the different foods, buying marigolds, and the procession to the cemetery.

Johnston, Tony. *My Mexico/México Mío.* Illus. F. John Sierra. New York: Putnam, 1996.

Illustrated bilingual poems about Mexico.

Johnston, Tony. *The Tale of Rabbit and Coyote.* Illus. Tomie DePaola. New York: Putnam, 1994.

In this Zapotec Indian legend from Oaxaca, Mexico, a farmer catches Rabbit eating his chiles. The captured Rabbit tricks Coyote into trading places with him. This leads to a chase and a series of tricks. Ultimately, Rabbit climbs to the Moon on a ladder. Coyote never finds the ladder that Rabbit has hidden, and that is why Coyote howls at the Moon.

Johnston, Tony. *Uncle Rain Cloud.* Illus. by Fabricio Vanden Broeck. Watertown, Mass.: Talewinds, 2001.

Carlos's Uncle Tomás has difficulty adjusting to life in Los Angeles because he cannot speak English. Uncle Tomás is more like his regular self when he tells Carlos stories of Mexico and tongue-twister gods—gods whose names are difficult to pronounce. When Uncle Tomás is embarrassed by Carlos translating during a meeting with Carlos's teacher, Uncle Tomás is finally forced to admit he is afraid to speak English, and Carlos admits he felt the same way too. Carlos starts teaching his uncle English words, and they agree that Uncle Tomás will teach Carlos the tales of the Mexican tongue-twister gods so that both will know twice as much.

Kent, Jack. *The Christmas Piñata.* New York: Parents' Magazine, 1975.

A cracked pot enviously eyes an uncracked pot's usefulness until he is used to make a piñata for *Las Posadas,* the reenactment of Mary and Joseph seeking shelter.

Kimmel, Eric A. *The Runaway Tortilla.* Illus. Randy Cecil. Delray Beach, Fla.: Winslow Press, 2000.

Inspired by *The Gingerbread Man,* the Runaway Tortilla runs away from Tía Lupe, famous for making light tortillas, and other Southwest animals and buckaroos.

Kimmel, Eric A. *The Witch's Face: A Mexican Tale.* Illus. Fabricio Vanden Broeck. New York: Holiday House, 1993.

A man traveling to Mexico City inadvertently spends the night at the house of three witches. The youngest one helps him escape and gives him instructions for how they can spend the rest of their lives together. Before they marry, he breaks those instructions and learns a valuable lesson.

Kleven, Elisa. *Hooray, a Piñata!* New York: Dutton, 1996.

Clara chooses a dog piñata for her birthday but grows very attached to it. She says "Hooray" when she receives another piñata for her birthday, and the children attending her party shout "Hooray" when they break it. A note about piñatas is included after the story.

Krull, Kathleen. *Maria Molina and the Day of the Dead.* Illus. Enrique O. Sanchez. New York: Macmillan, 1994.

After celebrating the Day of the Dead in a Mexican cemetery, Maria and her family move to the United States. Now they will celebrate Halloween, but Maria is worried that no one will honor their dead relatives because they cannot visit their graves. The family honors them with the *ofrenda,* or altar, in their apartment. Includes recipes for Pan de los Muertos/Bread of the Dead.

Lachtman, Ofelia Dumas. *Pepita Talks Twice/Pepita Habla Dos Veces.* Illus. Alex Pardo DeLange. Houston: Piñata Books, 1995.

Bilingual Pepita always translates for everyone without complaint until she realizes that it is very time-consuming. She decides to speak only English so that she won't have to speak twice, but she soon discovers how valuable it is to speak two languages.

Lasky, Kathryn. *Days of the Dead.* Illus. Christopher G. Knight. New York: Hyperion, 1994.

Through photographs, this children's book depicts the activities in a town where family members come from near and far to honor a dead couple on the Day of the Dead. Though some of the information is personal, much of the text applies to many Mexican Day of the Dead celebrations. Brief but more detailed information on specific topics, such as butterflies, appears at the end.

Levy, Janice. *The Spirit of Tío Fernando/El Espíritu de Tío Fernando.* Illus. by Morella Fuenmayor. Morton Grove, Ill.: Albert Whitman, 1995.

In this bilingual picture book, a young boy remembers his favorite uncle on the first Day of the Dead celebration without him by building an altar, going to the market, watching a *pastorela* (a play), and going to the cemetery, where he hopes Tío Fernando will know they have remembered him.

Libura, Krystyna. *What the Aztecs Told Me.* Toronto: Groundwood Books, 1997.

This picture book illustrates the daily lives of the Aztecs as recorded by Friar Bernardino. The drawings are from *The Florentine Codex*.

Linse, Barbara. *Art of the Folk: Mexican Heritage through Arts and Crafts for Boys and Girls.* Larkspur, Calif.: Arts' Books, 1980.

Divided up by state, this how-to book contains Mexican crafts for children.

Lomas Garza, Carmen. *Family Pictures/Cuadros de Familia.* San Francisco: Children's Book Press, 1990.

A collection of paintings depicting scenes from this Latina artist's childhood. Each painting includes her memories on its theme in English and Spanish. This collection includes *Las Posadas*, the reenactment of Mary and Joseph seeking shelter, and tamales.

Lomas Garza, Carmen. *In My Family/En Mi Familia.* San Francisco: Children's Book Press, 1996.

The second collection of paintings depicting this Latina artist's childhood. Each painting includes her memories on its theme in both English and Spanish. This collection includes empanadas, a healer (*curandera*), La Llorona (the weeping woman), and the Virgin of Guadalupe.

Lomas Garza, Carmen. *Magic Windows/Ventanas Mágicas.* San Francisco: Children's Book Press, 1999.

The beauty of *papel picado* (cut-paper art) is seen in this Pura Belpré Award–winning book. Each piece reflects a part of Lomas Garza's experience growing up, family, or Mexican heritage. The accompanying text also includes technical information about each piece.

Lomas Garza, Carmen. *Making Magic Windows: Creating Papel Picado/Cut-Paper Art with Carmen Lomas Garza.* San Francisco: Children's Book Press, 1999.

This source provides instructions and patterns for making *papel picado* (cut-paper art).

Luenn, Nancy. *A Gift for Abuelita: Celebrating the Day of the Dead/Un Regalo para Abuelita: En Celebración del Día de los Muertos.* Illus. Robert Chapman. Flagstaff, Ariz.: Rising Moon, 1998.

Rosita spends a lot of time with her grandmother. When her grandmother dies, Rosita wonders what she can make for her for Day of the Dead until she thinks of the perfect gift.

Machado, Ana Maria. *Niña Bonita.* Illus. Rosana Faría. Brooklyn: Kane/Miller Book Publishers, 1996.

A white rabbit envies a little girl's black skin and keeps asking her how she got her beautiful color until the little girl's mother answers her. The white rabbit finds a black spouse and has rabbits in all different shades of black and white. This story embraces the African heritage of many Caribbean countries.

MacMillan, Dianne M. *Mexican Independence Day and Cinco de Mayo.* Springfield, N.J.: Enslow Publishers, 1997.

This book for children covers both the history and festivities of Mexican Independence Day and Cinco de Mayo. There is historical information on Mexican independence, Benito Juárez, and the Battle of Puebla.

Mathew, Sally Schofer. *The Sad Night: The Story of an Aztec Victory and a Spanish Loss.* New York: Clarion, 1994.

The glory of the Aztecs and how they defeated Cortés is depicted in this picture book.

McConnie Zapafer, Beatriz. *Fiesta!* Illus. José Ortega. New York: Simon & Schuster Books for Young Readers, 1992.

A Colombian family now living in the United States prepares for a fiesta. Most Latin American towns have a fiesta for their patron saint, and this fiesta for all Hispanics includes a parade, a greased-pole climbing contest, and food.

Menard, Valerie. *Latino Holiday Book: From Cinco de Mayo to Día de los Muertos—the Celebrations and Traditions of Hispanic-Americans.* New York: Marlowe & Company, 2000.

This is a very complete resource on various Latino holidays for the adult reader.

Milord, Susan. *¡México! 40 Activities to Experience Mexico Past & Present.* Illus. Michael Kline. Charlotte, Vt.: Williamson Publishing, 1999.

Activities and background information are available in this source.

Mohr, Nicholasa, and Antonio Martorell. *The Song of el Coqui and Other Tales of Puerto Rico.* New York: Viking, 1995.

Each of the three folktales in this picture book "exemplifies one of the three most important culture groups in Puerto Rico."

Mora, Pat. *The Bakery Lady/La Señora de la Panadería.* Illus. Pablo Torrecilla. Trans. Gabriela Baeza Ventura and Pat Mora. Houston: Piñata Books, 2001.

Mónica lives with her brother and her grandparents above their bakery. She dreams about becoming a baker and is very proud of the apron she received for Christmas. She also longs to find the doll inside the Kings' Ring for the feast of the Three Kings. When she finds it, she is thrilled that she will give the *fiesta* (party) in February for her friends. With help, she is able to prepare for the *fiesta.*

Mora, Pat. *A Birthday Basket for Tía.* Illus. Cecily Lang. New York: Macmillan, 1992.

Not sure what to get her great-aunt for her birthday, Cecilia puts different things that mean something to the two of them in one basket.

Mora, Pat. *Confetti: Poems for Children.* Illus. Enrique O. Sanchez. New York: Lee & Low, 1996.

Illustrated poems by Mora. Many incorporate Spanish words. The glossary contains pronunciations and definitions.

Mora, Pat. *Delicious Hullabaloo/Pachanga Deliciosa.* Illus. Francisco X. Mora. Trans. Alba Nora Martínez and Pat Mora. Houston: Piñata Books, 1998.

In verse, this story tells how the animals prepare for a night filled with food, family, and friends.

Mora, Pat. *The Night the Moon Fell: A Maya Myth.* Illus. Domi. Toronto: Douglas & McIntyre, 2000.

In conjunction with the artist's signature style, Mora retells the Mayan tale about when the Moon dropped from the sky, fell into the ocean, and found a way to get back.

Mora, Pat. *The Rainbow Tulip.* Illus. Elizabeth Sayles. New York: Viking, 1999.

When all the girls need a tulip costume for May Day, Stella is very proud that each petal of her skirt is a different color. When she arrives at the parade, everyone else's tulip costume is only one color. This is Mora's mother's story, which reflects the bicultural experience and what it feels like to be different.

Mora, Pat. *Tomás and the Library Lady.* Illus. Raul Colón. New York: Knopf, 1997.

Tomás and his family are migrant workers. His grandfather is a great storyteller and takes Tómas to the library, where the librarian nurtures his reading. Each night Tómas goes home and tells the stories he reads to his family. This is based on Tómas Rivera, chancellor at the University of California–Riverside.

Mora, Pat, and Charles Ramírez Berg. *The Gift of the Poinsettia/El Regalo de la Flor de Nochebuena.* Illus. Daniel Lechón. Houston: Piñata Books, 1995.

This bilingual book tells the story of a young boy in a small Mexican town who worries that he does not have a gift for the baby Jesus during *Las Posadas* (the reenactment of Mary and Joseph seeking shelter). As the book covers each day of *Las Posadas,* many Latino foods and traditions are mentioned, such as piñatas, *papel picado* (cut-paper art), tamales, and *farolitos* (small lanterns). Songs in English and Spanish for *Las Posadas* are included with music.

Mora, Pat, ed. *Love to Mamá: A Tribute to Mothers.* Illus. Paula S. Barragán M. New York: Lee & Low, 2001.

Full-page illustrations accompany the wonderful poems written by Latino poets about mothers and grandmothers.

Muñoz Ryan, Pam. *Mice and Beans.* Illus. Joe Cepeda. New York: Scholastic, 2001.

Rosa María is hosting her youngest granddaughter's birthday party. While she is busy making Latino food and getting the piñata, she is also busy trying to catch a mouse. Little does she know that she is getting help preparing for the party. A recipe for Rosa María's Rice and Beans appears on the book's back cover.

Orozco, José-Luis. *De Colores and Other Latin-American Folk Songs for Children.* Illus. Elisa Kleven. New York: Dutton, 1994.

Music and lyrics are included in this illustrated collection of traditional and original folk songs for children in English and Spanish. Sound recordings available.

Orozco, José-Luis. *Diez Deditos and Other Play Rhymes and Action Songs from Latin America.* Illus. Elisa Kleven. New York: Dutton, 1997.

Music and lyrics are included in this illustrated collection of traditional and original folk songs for children in English and Spanish. Sound recordings available.

Palacios, Argentina. *¡Viva México! A Story of Benito Juárez and Cinco de Mayo.* Illus. Howard Berelson. Austin, Tex.: Raintree/Steck-Vaughn, 1993.

Biography of Benito Juárez, who was president of Mexico during the Battle of Puebla.

Paulsen, Gary. *The Tortilla Factory.* Illus. Ruth Wright Paulsen. San Diego, Calif.: Harcourt, 1995.

The process of making a tortilla is illustrated— from planting the seed to eating the tortilla to starting the whole process all over again.

Perl, Lila. *Piñatas and Paper Flowers: Holidays of the Americas in English and Spanish/Piñatas y Flores de Papel: Fiestas de las Americas en Ingles y Español.* Illus. Victoria de Larrea. Spanish version by Alma Flor Ada. New York: Clarion, 1983.

This bilingual book gives brief descriptions of several Hispanic holidays as they are celebrated in North, Central, and South America: New Year, Three Kings' Day, Carnival and Easter, St. John the Baptist Day, Columbus Day, Halloween, the Festival of the Sun, and Christmas.

Perry, Michael. *Daniel's Ride.* Illus. Lee Ballard. San Francisco: Free Will Press, 2001.

Daniel's big brother just bought a 1963 Chevrolet Impala convertible. After a remarkable day of driving around, he promises Daniel that the "low rider" is his when he graduates from high school with plans to go to college.

Politi, Leo. *Pedro, the Angel of Olvera Street.* New York: Scribner, 1946.

Pedro sings like an angel and loves Olvera Street. Readers join him and celebrate Christmas, Las Posadas procession (the reenactment of Mary and Joseph seeking shelter), and a piñata.

Reiser, Lynn. *Tortillas and Lullabies/Tortillas y Cancioncitas.* New York: Greenwillow, 1998.

Three generations of women are depicted making tortillas, gathering flowers, washing, and singing lullabies in this warm story.

Riehecky, Janet. *Cinco de Mayo.* Illus. Krystyna Stasiak. Chicago: Children's Press, 1993.

Maria tries to help with the traditional Cinco de Mayo preparations but breaks something every time. Her mother encourages her to enter the Cinco de Mayo drawing contest at the library. She draws the different members of her family preparing for Cinco de Mayo, wins the contest, and breaks the Cinco de Mayo piñata!

Rohmer, Harriet. *Uncle Nacho's Hat/El Sombrero del Tío Nacho.* Illus. Veg Reisberg. San Francisco: Children's Book Press, 1989.

In this Nicaraguan folktale, Uncle Nacho's niece gives him a new hat, but he cannot seem to get rid of his old one.

Rohmer, Harriet, ed. *Honoring Our Ancestors: Stories and Pictures by Fourteen Artists.* San Francisco: Children's Book Press, 1999.

Artists of diverse ethnic backgrounds contribute a piece of art and written text honoring their ancestors, blood relations and otherwise.

Rohmer, Harriet, ed. *Just Like Me: Stories and Self-Portraits by Fourteen Artists.* San Francisco: Children's Book Press, 1997.

Artists of diverse ethnic backgrounds share their self-portraits and the stories behind them.

Salinas, Bobbi. *Indo-Hispanic Folk Art Traditions I: Christmas and Other Year-Round Activities.* Alameda, Calif.: Piñata Publications, 1994.

Everything you need for a complete program or display. This bilingual book contains instructions for making or preparing a nativity scene, piñata, *Ojos de Dios, papel picado* (cut-paper art), *aguinaldos* (gifts), *Las Posadas* (the reenactment of Mary and Joseph seeking shelter), Tree of Life, Huichol yarn painting, and luminarias, or *farolitos* (small lanterns). Recipes include Three Kings' Ring Bread, *buñuelos* (cookies), sopapillas, *atole* (a drink), and chocolate. There is a vocabulary list in both languages and photo plates.

Salinas, Bobbi. *Indo-Hispanic Folk Art Traditions II: The Day of the Dead and Other Year-Round Activities.* Alameda, Calif.: Piñata Publications, 1994.

Everything you need for the Day of the Dead. This bilingual book contains instructions for altars, toys, skeletons and skulls, crafts, foods, and folk theater and dance. There is a vocabulary list in both languages and photo plates.

Salinas, Bobbi. *The Three Little Pigs/Los Tres Cerdos: Nacho, Tito, and Miguel.* Alameda, Calif.: Piñata Publications, 1998.

The art and text in this nonviolent Chicano version of the traditional folktale reflect Latino culture and heritage that the children will recognize and are a source of pride.

Señor Cat's Romance and Other Favorite Stories from Latin America. Retold by Lucía M. González. Illus. Lulu Delacre. New York: Scholastic, 1997.

After hearing different versions of different Latino folktales, González has retold them in this illustrated collection. Each retelling includes background information about the folktale.

Silverthorne, Elizabeth. *Fiesta! Mexico's Great Celebrations.* Brookfield, Conn.: Millbrook Press, 1992.

This children's introduction to Mexico's religious, patriotic, and other celebrations includes fiesta descriptions as well as a few crafts and recipes.

Slate, Joseph. *The Secret Stars.* Illus. Felipe Davalos. New York: Marshall Cavendish, 1998.

Pepe and Sila worry that the Three Kings will not find them because of the heavy rain. Their grandmother tells them they must sleep or the Three Kings will not come. Wrapped in their grandmother's quilt, Pepe, Sila, and their grandmother sleep, dream, and fly through the night, discovering stars everywhere. They awaken in the morning and see that the Three Kings did find their way.

Soto, Gary. *Big Bushy Mustache.* Illus. Joe Cepeda. New York: Knopf, 1998.

Ricky wonders why people always say he looks like his mother and never say he looks like his father. When his teacher hands out props for the Cinco de Mayo play, Ricky volunteers to wear the mustache that looks like his father's. He sneaks it out of the classroom only to lose it on the way home. What will he wear for the play?

Soto, Gary. *Chato and the Party Animals.* Illus. Susan Guevara. New York: Putnam, 2000.

In this sequel to *Chato's Kitchen,* Chato throws a party for one of his homeboys.

Soto, Gary. *Chato's Kitchen.* Illus. Susan Guevara. New York: Putnam, 1995.

Chato and his barrio cat friend look forward to having their new mice neighbors for dinner in this funny story that includes a few cool Spanish words.

Soto, Gary. *Neighborhood Odes.* Illus. David Diaz. San Diego, Calif.: Harcourt Brace Jovanovich, 1992.

Poetry anthology for older children.

Soto, Gary. *Snapshots from the Wedding.* Illus. Stephanie García. New York: Putnam, 1997.

A Latino wedding is depicted in this picture book illustrated with Sculpy clay and other objects.

Soto, Gary. *Too Many Tamales.* Illus. Ed Martinez. New York: Putnam, 1993.

While making tamales with her family on Christmas Eve, Maria tries on and loses her mother's diamond ring. Fearing that it fell into the *masa* (dough), Maria and her cousins start eating the tamales, hoping to find it.

Spieler, Marlena. *Flavors of Mexico: Fresh, Simple Twists on Classical Regional Dishes.* Los Angeles: Lowell House, 1991.

This Mexican cookbook also includes information on foods and ingredients used in its recipes.

Stevens, Jan Romero. *Carlos and the Cornfield.* Flagstaff, Ariz.: Rising Moon, 1995.

Carlos's father offers to pay him for planting corn. Once he starts working, he decides to find ways to finish quicker. But when the corn begins to sprout, it is obvious that his work was not consistent.

Stevens, Jan Romero. *Twelve Lizards Leaping: A New "Twelve Days of Christmas."* Illus. Christine Mau. Flagstaff, Ariz.: Rising Moon, 1999.

Included in this Southwest version of the traditional song are three horned toads, ten tamales steaming, and five turquoise rings.

Tabor, Nancy María Grande. *El Gusto del Mercado Mexicano/A Taste of the Mexican Market.* Watertown, Mass.: Charlesbridge, 1996.

Different foods are introduced in this trip to the Mexican market.

Tabor, Nancy María Grande. *Somos un Arco Iris/We Are a Rainbow.* Watertown, Mich.: Charlesbridge, 1995.

This bilingual book explores the differences between the United States and Latino countries and demonstrates that the children share many similarities.

Tompert, Ann. *The Silver Whistle.* Illus. Beth Peck. New York: Macmillan, 1988.

It's the day before Christmas and the day of the annual holiday festival. Miguel is anxious to sell all the whistles he has made so that he can buy a silver whistle for the Procession of Gifts at the cathedral. When he is unable to buy it, he wonders what to do.

Trenchard, Kathleen. *Mexican Papercutting: Simple Techniques for Creating Colorful Cut-Paper Projects.* Asheville, N.C.: Lark Books, 1998.

This is an excellent source written for adults about Mexican paper cutting. There are instructions for using *papel picado* (cut-paper art) in a number of items.

Vázquez, Sarah. *Cinco de Mayo.* Austin, Tex.: Raintree/Steck-Vaughn, 1999.

From the World of Holidays series, this children's title contains historical information on the Battle of Puebla and modern-day celebrations. Though focusing on Cinco de Mayo, this book contains chapters on costumes, music, dance, food, and other Mexican and Mexican American traditions.

Viesti, Joe, and Diane Hall. *Celebrate! In Central America.* New York: Lothrop, Lee & Shepard, 1997.

This photographic essay includes short sections focusing on unique celebrations in Central America. Includes sections on Día de los Muertos (Day of the Dead) in Santiago de Sacatepéquez, Guatemala, where huge tissue-paper kites are flown, and Columbus Day in Puerto Limón, Costa Rica, less than a mile from where Columbus landed on his final voyage to the Americas.

Wakefield, Charito Calvachi. *Navidad Latinoamericana/ Latin American Christmas.* Lancaster, Pa.: Latin American Creations Publishing, 1997.

Completely bilingual, this resource includes Christmas carols, *La Novena de Navidad* (or Nine Days of Prayers) before Christmas, Christmas traditions in Latin American countries, and a CD.

Wing, Natasha. *Jalapeño Bagels.* Illus. Robert Casilla. New York: Atheneum, 1996.

Half Mexican and half Jewish, Pablo cannot decide what food to take to school for International Day.

Winter, Jeanette. *Josefina.* San Diego, Calif.: Harcourt, 1996.

Inspired by Mexican folk artist Josefina Aguilar, who makes painted clay figures, this book serves as a counting book and an introduction to Latino folk art and culture.

Diana Borrego has thirteen years of experience in children's services and is currently at the San Jose Public Library. Originally from Ciudad Juarez, Mexico, she came to the United States in 1961 and earned her M.L.S. degree in 1986 from San Jose State University. She is active in Bibliotecas Para La Gente, her local REFORMA chapter.

Ana-Elba Pavon is the Children's Services Manager at the San Francisco Public Library's Mission Branch, which contains the city's largest Spanish collection and hosts weekly Spanish and bilingual story times. As a library student, she was the Latino researcher for ALA Graphics' Celebrate America's Diversity. Ana is active in Bibliotecas Para La Gente, her local REFORMA chapter. She earned her M.L.I.S. degree from the University of California at Berkeley in 1992.